Everyday Life
of the
Etruscans

A nineteenth-century reconstruction of the town of Sutri (Sutrium)

Everyday Life of

THE ETRUSCANS

ELLEN MACNAMARA

Drawings by Eva Wilson

to Peggy

from

Ellen Macnamara.

B. T. BATSFORD LTD
LONDON

G. P. PUTNAMS' SONS
NEW YORK

To my nephews RORY *and* JAMES MACNAMARA,
who have visited some Etruscan sites with me.

First published 1973
Text © Ellen Macnamara, 1973
Illustrations © B. T. Batsford Ltd, 1973
ISBN 0 7134 1691 2
LCC NO.: 73-76715
AMERICAN SBN 399-20367-2
Printed and bound in Great Britain by
William Clowes & Sons, Limited
London, Beccles and Colchester
for the publishers
B. T. BATSFORD LTD
4 Fitzhardinge Street, London WIH OAH
G. P. PUTNAMS' SONS
200 Madison Avenue, New York NY 10016

CONTENTS

ACKNOWLEDGEMENTS

I wish to thank two of my teachers, Professor A. Momigliano and Professor C. M. Robertson, for their great kindness in commenting upon parts of the script of this book. I am also deeply indebted to Professor D. Strong, Doctor J. Close-Brooks and Doctor A. Snodgrass for their valued criticisms and to my friends Katherine Butler, Fiona Campbell, Michael Sandwith and Jane Ridley for reading and improving the script. I also wish to thank Mr Kemmis Betty, Mrs Hughes and Mrs Moore of B. T. Batsford Ltd, together with Mrs Wilson, for their help, encouragement and, above all, for their patience.

The Author and Publisher would also like to thank the trustees of the museums whose exhibits are illustrated in this book and whose names appear in the captions; Alinari and the Mansell Collection for figs 8, 22, 24, 30, 35, 36, 40, 44, 51, 64, 65, 71 (Alinari-Anderson), 74, 75, 82, 85, 95, 97, 98, 101, 102, 103 and 112; the Ciba Foundation, Churchills and Dr Nieppi Modona for fig 3; Editions d'Art Albert Skira for figs 46, 47, 49, 50, 107 and jacket; Dr Martin Hürlimann, Switzerland, for fig 41; Lerice, Rome (Moretti: *Nuovi monumenti della pittura etrusca*, 1966) for fig 48; L. von Matt, Switzerland, for figs 7 and 94; Touring Club Italiano (*Conosci L'Italia Vol. IV*, 1960) for fig 87. Figs 1, 9, 11, 13, 23 are adapted from the same source; University of Chicago Press (Richardson: *The Etruscans, their Art and Civilization*, 1964) for fig 28. Fig 109 is adapted from the same source. The frontispiece and figs 14 and 15 are from Canina: *Etruria Marittima*, 1849.

THE ILLUSTRATIONS

PREFACE

Ancient Etruria, the beautiful region of Italy lying between Florence and Rome, has always attracted visitors eager to see the fine stretch of Mediterranean coastline, the countryside with terraced hillsides covered in vines and the enchanting towns, famous for their prodigious store of Medieval and Renaissance works of art. There are, however, traces of an earlier culture centred in this region, and some travellers may have become aware that it was the Etruscans who first carved the landscape into a form still familiar to this day. It was the Etruscans who founded a town upon the hilltop of Fiesole, overlooking Florence, and placed a city on the magnificent citadel of rock at Orvieto, which stands high above the modern *autostrada* leading south to Rome.

For this was the homeland of the Etruscan city-states. Some of the Etruscan cities had already reached a high prosperity by the seventh century BC, whilst others retained their power down to the completion of the Roman conquest during the third century BC. Even after this date, the Etruscans continued to produce art in a local manner and the language was still used in the first century BC. During these seven centuries, Greek civilization reached its highest achievement and was represented in Italy by the colonial cities of the south, and the Republic of Rome grew from a small state into the greatest power of the Mediterranean world.

This background might suggest a fully historic period with a wide range of literature available to us, in which contemporary witnesses describe many aspects, both abstract and material, of Etruscan society. Unfortunately, however, the vast majority of Etruscan writings have not survived and what inscriptions we possess and can interpret with certainty provide us with little general information and few glimpses into their daily lives. For written testimony, we must mainly rely upon the works of

Greek and Roman authors, whose interests and loyalties were concentrated elsewhere and who were often writing long after the events they describe.

These sources do give us a precious outline of historic events which affected the Etruscans, and some comments upon their way of life, but little was added about the internal affairs of Etruria nor of the ordinary activities of the people. Thus it has been principally from a study of the archaeological evidence that, during the last hundred and fifty years, a picture has been built up of the differing character of the cities of Etruria, of the art and general culture of the Etruscans and some details of their day-to-day life. Each year this knowledge is increased by excavation in the cities and cemeteries of Etruria, with all the careful recording of the sites and detailed study of the monuments, together with the pottery, metalwork and other finds. Meanwhile, other methods and disciplines combine to enlarge our understanding of Etruscan life with further research into the grammar and vocabulary of the language, and its relationship with other languages; fresh assessments of the Etruscan achievement in the arts; new enquiries into their racial affinities, their religion and many other aspects of their society.

Using these very different types of evidence, a general picture and some particular aspects of Etruscan society may be described but the gaps in our knowledge are vast. We cannot yet resolve the riddle of the origin of the Etruscans nor is the language fully understood. Since references in the written sources to the more abstract elements of Etruscan life are rare and often vague, it is easier to approach them primarily through the more tangible evidence of the monuments and the objects which have come down to us. Using all the *minutiae* of modern research, the student must try to distil the character of the civilization from these artistic and technical achievements and, from the written sources, evoke the personality of the people and thus imagine the life led by the Etruscans.

Note

† *Daggers in the text indicate that information in the preceding paragraph was derived from ancient authors. Details of these sources are given on p. 207. Numbered text notes are explained on p. 193.*

The archaeological background

Modern Tuscany still bears a form of the Latin name for the Etruscans, though the geographical boundaries have altered from those of ancient Etruria. The homeland of the Etruscan city-states lay within modern Tuscany and the northern part of Lazio (1) (notes, p. 193) and was roughly bounded by the Arno to the north and to the east and south by the Tiber. To the west lies the Tyrrhenian Sea, called by a Greek form of the Etruscan name, and here the Etruscans held the small off-shore islands, including Elba (2) (*1, 9* and *11*). From north to south, this region is seldom more than two hundred and fifty kilometres (one hundred and fifty-six miles) and, from east to west, it is usually less than one hundred and fifty kilometres (ninety-four miles), so that the total area may be broadly compared with that of Wales. These boundaries changed from time to time; as will be described below, the Etruscans, in the course of their history, expanded their power beyond the limits of their homeland.

The geography, climate and ecology of this region were favourable to settlement, though in early times the forests must have proved formidable barriers and the periodic flooding of rivers has been a persistent problem. Generally, the rock of the southern half of the region is of volcanic origin; it is called 'tuff' and is made of the densely packed layers of ash, once flung from the volcanoes, whose craters now have become the lakes of Bolsena, Vico and Bracciano. With the exception of the crater rims, which ring the three lakes, and of the Tolfa Hills and Monte Soratte (both of which have a different geological formation), much of the southern region of Etruria is a broad plateau with gently rolling hills. This plateau is cut by the

1 Map of the east and central Mediterranean

pattern of abrupt ravines and gullies, which have been channelled through the soft rock by the water-courses. These rivers and streams drain in three directions, either to the Tiber to the east and south or, westwards, into the Tyrrhenian Sea.

The part of Etruria lying to the north of a line drawn roughly from the Paglia to the Fiora Valley has a wider landscape. Geologically, it is composed of sandstones and limestones and has broad valleys and groups of hills, some of which reach quite imposing heights. This region may be subdivided into two areas: there is a western zone of hills, into which are cut the valleys of rivers flowing either to the sea or, northwards, into the Arno; to the east, there lies the fertile basin of the upper Tiber and its tributaries with their rich soil, which was to become the best agricultural district of Etruria.

The two principal metal-bearing regions of Etruria lay near the Tyrrhenian coast. One was centred in the Tolfa Hills, lying to the north of the Tiber mouth. The second was the mining zone along the north coast around the promontory of Piombino; this included the large deposits of metal ores lying among the Colline Metallifere and the iron ore of Elba.

Some broader geographical knowledge is required to understand the development which occurred in this region. A coastal plain runs north from the Arno mouth but, beyond this, the Apennines and Ligurian Alps reach down to the sea and present a barrier which was impassable for practical purposes in the Etruscan period. To the north and east of the middle Arno Valley, however, many small river valleys cut into the spine of the Apennines, which is here neither very high nor wide; from the watershed, other rivers run down into the lower Po Valley, thus forming routes which were constantly used from the Bronze Age onwards. Although the great valley of the Po must have had considerable areas of swamp, the river links the lower Po Valley with the Italian Lakes and their Alpine valleys, while the valley of the Adige leads northwards to the Brenner Pass.

The valley of the Tiber, with its navigable river, both united and divided Etruria from Umbria to the east and Lazio to the south; as frequently occurs, the river proved to be a political boundary, while it was at the same time a cultural link. Etruscan culture crossed it, and it is not always easy to be sure just where the political divisions lay; nevertheless, the

Tiber was a basic boundary between peoples. To the south, routes to the rich plain of Campania led through southern Lazio, either along the coastal plain or past Palestrina (Praeneste), and on down the valleys of the Sacco and Liri.

The coastline of Etruria has long, open stretches, cut by the promontories of Monte Argentario, Talamone, the hills to the west of Vetulonia and the promontory of Piombino. This coastline has altered in some places since antiquity, most notably in the area between Vetulonia and Roselle, where silting has filled a large bay or lagoon. Good natural harbours are rare along this coast but a sheltered beach on which a ship could be pulled up out of the water remained for centuries a good enough alternative. Throughout their early history, the Etruscans were renowned sailors and the sea was a highway uniting them with the other peoples of the Mediterranean.

It is necessary to go back to the Bronze Age in order to describe several strands which were to play a part in the creation of the Etruscan community and to understand the arguments surrounding the vexed question of its origin. There is evidence for a flourishing Early Bronze Age culture in northern Lazio and Tuscany, already using the local copper and, perhaps, tin ore, the two alloys which are used in the manufacture of tin bronze. It is rare to find these two ores in the same region, and the long tradition of local bronzework reflects both the availability of these materials and the skills this aroused in generation after generation of metalworkers.

By the time of the Middle Bronze Age, though Tuscany was already in touch with the people living in the lower Po Valley, the western side of the peninsula was hardly affected by the influences which were then spreading along the great corridor of the Adriatic between central Europe and Greece. At this time, mainland Greece was enjoying the final phases of the sophisticated Mycenaean civilization with its walled cities, fine palaces and tombs of kings, whose legends survive in the Homeric poems. There are many stories of Mycenaean sailors and Minoans from Crete voyaging in the west Mediterranean and sometimes even settling in Italy. Such voyages are confirmed by the presence of imports from the Aegean which have been found in the south of the peninsula, in Sicily, on the Lipari Islands and, on the west coast, as far north as Ischia (an island lying off the Bay of Naples), and even a few fragments of pottery from Luni, near Blera, some sixty kilometres (thirty-seven miles) north-west of Rome. Our knowledge of west central Italy at this time is still meagre and may well give too slight an impression of contacts with the Aegean area.

About the end of the thirteenth and during the twelfth century BC (3), the Mycenaean civilization underwent a series of disasters, in which many of the cities were destroyed, probably by land raiders from the north. This collapse is associated with a large-scale movement of peoples throughout the east Mediterranean area; the Hittite Empire fell, the cities of the Levant were sacked and the borders of Egypt were attacked by the Peoples of the Sea. By about 1050 BC, despite having learned the use of iron, Greece had entered a Dark Age and Italy, in her turn, became isolated from the more advanced cultures of the Aegean and east Mediterranean. Although there are some signs of the renewal of such contacts in Sicily and Calabria, for the next two and a half centuries practically all the important new ideas entered Italy from the north-east and north, a region which was then still enjoying a flourishing Late Bronze Age culture.

Such a change of balance naturally affected the development of the cultures of Italy. The Italian Middle Bronze Age had seen a number of regional cultures, notably those centred in Emilia, Apulia and east Sicily but the whole length of the peninsula had been united to a remarkable degree in the Apennine Culture. The people of the Apennine Culture almost certainly spoke an Indo-European language and they buried the corpses of their dead. (This funerary style is known as 'inhumation'.) Traditions deriving from the Apennine Culture continued over wide areas of the peninsula, whilst with the gradual breakdown of sea communications in the Mediterranean, a new pattern of cultures emerged in Italy.

Among the important innovations at this time was the arrival in Italy of the funerary rite of cremation, usually by burning the corpse upon a pyre before gathering and disposing of the ashes. It is still uncertain whence and precisely when this tradition entered Italy but it is known that people using cremation were settled in the south Alpine valleys by the thirteenth century BC. However, the most significant evidence of the new rite may be seen in the spread of a culture which archaeologists call proto- or pre-Villanovan; the people of the proto-Villanovan Culture used a distinctive type of pottery urn in which to bury the ashes of their dead and they placed these in groups, or urnfields.

The bronze objects found with these urns help us to date the proto-Villanovan period from the twelfth to about the end of the tenth century BC. Of the major proto-Villanovan urnfields known to us, one lies north of the Po River, examples are scattered over central Italy, including our region, and an important urnfield has been excavated at Timmari, in Lucania, at the south of the peninsula. Other early urnfields are known in the south, including sites on the Lipari Islands and Sicily, which must have been reached by sea. These urnfields may be the result of a common tradition, stemming from the north, or, perhaps, a second current of people using cremation reached the shores of Italy from the east Mediterranean. In any case, the culture which produced the widely dispersed urnfields in the south of Italy was largely absorbed into the local forms and it was in the north, in the Po Valley and especially in Lombardy, at Este and among the Villanovans that cremation remained the dominant rite.

The Villanovan Culture is called after a site near Bologna where it was first recognized during the last century: this is just a modern archaeological term, denoting a certain group of cultural traits, which are habitually found together. It now seems likely that the Villanovan Culture originated in Emilia and spread into Tuscany, parts of Umbria and Lazio, with offshoots reaching Campania. Since it is growing increasingly clear that the Villanovans formed a major part of what was to become the Etruscan community, a short description of their culture is necessary here.

The Villanovan period has been divided into two principal phases, Villanovan I and Villanovan II, dating approximately to the ninth and eighth centuries BC. The Villanovans do not generally seem to have settled at the same sites in Tuscany and northern Lazio as their predecessors, the proto-Villanovans, but the Villanovans frequently occupied the favourable sites, which later became great Etruscan cities. The Villanovans were warriors with fine arms and armour and are sometimes depicted mounted upon horses; they were also farmers and had wheeled vehicles. They exploited the metal resources of the region and were very skilled bronzesmiths; they were sailors, who not only traded with Sardinia but probably also sailed along the west coast of the peninsula as far as Sicily and perhaps even farther afield in the west Mediterranean. The graves, which are our chief source of information about the Villanovans, show no great distinctions of wealth and the women were as richly equipped as the men.

The number of people living together in a Villanovan community was quite small; no complete Villanovan village has yet been excavated but it has been estimated from the number of contemporary graves that from three hundred to six hundred people lived at Veii, probably in groups of huts on the plateau, which later became the site of an Etruscan city. We know what these huts were like both from excavated ground plans and from the delightful pottery models, which the Villanovans sometimes used as urns for the ashes of their dead (2). The excavated ground plans show the position of post-holes and bedding trenches for the timbers of the walls; the huts were oval, or rectangular with rounded corners and examples of up to ten metres (eleven yards) in length are known. The hut-urns show many variations, though they may represent the smaller huts as yet only known from southern Lazio. The door is usually shown at the gable end of the hut and is sometimes flanked by free-standing poles, forming a small porch. The walls were made of wattle and daubed clay; a window is occasionally shown in the models and a vent hole, under the beams of the gable, allowed smoke to escape from the hut. The roof was thatched and overlaid with poles to hold this in position and

2 *Pottery urn in the form of a model hut*

the ends of these poles are often shown carved with the heads of birds. The most famous hut, contemporary with Villanovan examples, was on the Palatine Hill of Rome; Roman tradition stated that here Romulus, the founder of the city, had lived and Roman piety preserved the hut into classical times. Modern excavation has unearthed hut foundations in the area.

Round the Villanovan habitation sites are grouped the cemeteries, from which much of our information comes so that they are of prime importance in interpreting the development of the culture. The form of the graves and the objects found together in each grave show how the burial practice and the personal possessions of the dead altered in the course of time, and these changing forms sometimes allow us to place the graves in a chronological sequence and even occasionally to suggest dates and historical inferences. The graves begin with the *pozzetto* type, or well grave; this is often in the form of a

3 Well grave from Monte S. Angelo, east of Lake Bracciano

round pit, which in some cases was lined with a dry-stone walling and covered with a stone slab (*3*). In this pit was placed the urn, containing the ashes of the dead, with a bowl serving as lid and it was accompanied by some of the possessions of the dead man or woman.

Cremation was not the only funerary rite in central Italy. The older rite of inhumation, or burial of the corpse, continued to be used in Umbria, southern Lazio and other districts, and during Villanovan II, and especially in northern Lazio, there was a general tendency towards inhumation in *fosse*, or trench graves, which were sometimes enlarged with a niche at the side to hold the grave goods. As we shall see, the change of funerary rite was not uniform in Etruria in later centuries.

The urns, in which the Villanovans buried the ashes of their dead, had a characteristic shape with a wide body, rounded shoulders and a high conical neck (*3*). They often had a single handle, set on the body, and were decorated with incised patterns of repeated geometric designs, including the maeander and the swastika. Both the urns and the domestic pottery, which was made of impure clay, fired brown/black, a fabric known as *impasto*, had patterns sometimes picked out in white or augmented with bronze studs. The domestic pottery had a wide variety of forms, showing the influence of both Apennine Culture and proto-Villanovan traditions.

There is a rich repertoire of contemporary bronze objects. They include arms and armour, horsegear and tools, knives and razors, cups and buckets, spindles and jewellery, above all, the long series of *fibulae* (brooches or safety-pins), whose ever-changing fashions provide the most significant examples of metalwork throughout the Italian Late Bronze and Early Iron Age. The typology of these bronzes, that is, the traditions and affiliations shown by their form and the manner in which they were worked, can help us understand what was taking place in northern Lazio and Tuscany at this time.

First, a few Villanovan I bronzes show influence derived from the Aegean area or the east Mediterranean, though this might spring from objects imported at an even earlier date. Secondly, they show a very strong and sustained influence from the north Alpine, upper Danubian and north Balkan regions; recent research has shown that these bronze types derive from many different areas and that trade, not migration, was involved. Among the most notable bronze forms adopted by the Villanovans from these regions are cups with repoussé decoration, belts of sheet bronze, often decorated with an engraved pattern related to the iconography used at that time in central Europe, swords with hilts ending in curled antennae and fine crested helmets and body armour (*4*).

Many of the bronzes, however, are purely Italic in type either of local forms or of styles developed in the other regions

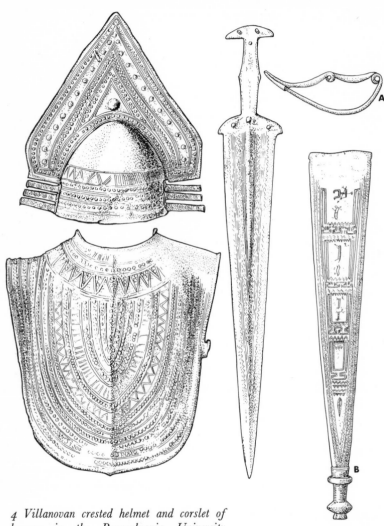

4 *Villanovan crested helmet and corslet of bronze in the Pennsylvania University Museum, Philadelphia*

5A Fibula *of Sicilian type.* B *Villanovan sword and sheath of bronze from Tarquinia*

of Italy. The *fibulae*, or brooches, generally demonstrate the strength of local traditions but some show links with Bologna and a Sicilian form, with two loops in a bent back and a long catch-plate, was widely copied by the Villanovans (*5A*).

Also from Sicily, where it had evolved from a mingling of Mycenaean and central European forms, came the characteristic Villanovan type of short sword with a T-shaped pommel, which also has been found in Calabria and which reached northern Lazio and Tuscany during the Villanovan I period (*5B*). It is possible that the new knowledge of iron technology also arrived from the south at this time.

Sicily appears to have learned the use of iron for tools by the tenth century BC and this knowledge must have been introduced from Greece or the east Mediterranean. However, these contacts remained very tenuous and, as regards the west central coast of Italy, they appear to have been indirect. Thus we may note the strong continuity shown throughout the Villanovan I and II periods in our region which suggests that no significant movement of people occurred here either in the ninth or eighth century BC. Further, we know of no direct contact between northern Lazio or Tuscany and the Aegean or east Mediterranean until the arrival of Greek pottery in the Geometric style and small trinkets of east Mediterranean type, which appear in northern Lazio at the beginning of Villanovan II, that is, early in the eighth century BC. But from this moment onwards, foreign goods appear more and more often in the Villanovan Culture of our region.

The division between the cultures using inhumation and cremation as their funerary rite during the Italian Late Bronze Age has already been stressed; this marks a deep cultural division, though not necessarily one of race. Language may also cross ethnic barriers but it, too, is a fundamental cultural trait. At the time when inscriptions begin to appear all over Italy, we may see a broad division of three linguistic regions. To the west are the non-Indo-European languages, including Sardinian, Ligurian and Etruscan; an Italic form of Indo-European is found along the spine of the Apennines and is represented by Latin and the dialects spoken by the Umbrians, Samnites and other peoples, whilst on the east coast Illyrian influence is found.

Early in the eighth century BC, Greek imports were beginning to appear among the Villanovans living in northern Lazio. Contemporary imports, notably trinkets from the east Mediterranean and Greek pottery cups in the Geometric style, have been found in Italic graves in Campania, including the native cemetery at Cuma (Cumae), just north of Naples. We do not know of anything dating as early as these objects from a colonial Greek or Phoenician context in Italy and we must therefore presume they represent a short period of trade before the Greeks began to found settlements.

We are told that the first Greek colony in Italy was at Cuma but that this was preceded by a settlement of Greeks on Ischia, the neighbouring offshore island on which Mycenaean pottery has come to light. This settlement was founded by Greeks from the island of Euboea and included a strong contingent from the city of Chalcis; this has recently been confirmed by the discovery and excavation of the colonial cemetery near Lacco Ameno on Ischia (Pithecusae).† (See p. 207.)

It is now clear that the settlement was founded before the middle of the eighth century BC; the graves contained not only Greek goods but bronzes, trinkets and pottery from the east Mediterranean and, significantly, imports from northern Lazio or Tuscany. Already by the end of the ninth century BC, the Euboean Greeks had established trading posts on the coast of the Levant; thence they brought goods from the east Mediterranean, both for their own enjoyment and to trade with their Italic neighbours. So, in the company of Greek pottery, objects from the east Mediterranean began to reach the Villanovans.

Apart from these new influences, Villanovan II contrasts sharply with the preceding period in the greatly increased use of iron. During the Villanovan I period of the ninth century BC, few weapons or tools were made of iron but this was becoming much more usual in the following century and, later, few weapons were of bronze. This development should be connected with Greek activity; the Greeks were in need of metal ores and must have offered the Villanovans a very lucrative trade, causing the exploitation of the local ores. It is significant that the settlement on Ischia was both the first in Italy and the farthest from Greece, suggesting that the Euboeans were at least as interested in trade as in finding new lands to colonize. Recently, remains of iron smelting have been found on the island and it has been shown that the ores were imported from Tuscany. It is this trade which must explain the increasing wealth of the Villanovans during the eighth century BC and the extraordinary purchasing power of the Etruscans in the succeeding period.

Other Greek states soon followed the example of the Euboeans and sent colonies to the west and, in the course of the next hundred years, many cities were founded along the coasts of southern Italy and Sicily. We have a series of foundation dates, based upon information given by Thucydides†; the key date is that of the foundation of the great Corinthian colony of Syracuse in 733 BC. By the end of the seventh century BC, a chain of Greek colonies ran from Taranto in Apulia, round the coasts of Lucania, Calabria and Campania as far north as Cuma, while in Sicily colonies were placed from Selinunte (Selinus) on the south coast, all round the east end of the island to Himera on the north coast. Three Phoenician colonies were grouped at the western end of the island and Carthage lay opposite on the coast of Africa.

It is not yet clear what part was played by the Phoenicians in opening up the western Mediterranean; possibly their predecessors, like the Mycenaeans, already knew the shipping routes to the west in the thirteenth century BC. The Greeks believed that the Phoenicians had reached the west Mediterranean before themselves in the colonizing age and the traditional date for the foundation of Carthage is 814 BC. No archaeological evidence has yet been found to support so early a date but the Phoenicians may at first have been primarily concerned with the exploitation of the metal ores of Spain. Certainly, they founded Motya, a colony on the small island of San Pantaleo off the west coast of Sicily, before the end of the eighth century BC and they were probably establishing permanent settlements on Sardinia at this time. Henceforth, they were in a position to trade directly with Etruria.

Neither the Greeks nor Phoenicians colonized the coast of northern Lazio and Tuscany, although it was by far the richest metal-bearing region of Italy, and metal ores were then sought for, as oil is today. The Villanovans must have been sufficiently numerous and organized to prevent the encroachment endured by the inhabitants of Apulia, Lucania, Calabria, Campania, Sicily and Sardinia. Their achievement had a long and deep effect upon the history of Italy.

2

The origin of the Etruscans

In the course of the seventh century BC, the inhabitants of Etruria learned to write and, since they wrote in Etruscan, it is safe to call the region and people by these names. Before this date, it is possible only to use archaeological terms given to certain local cultures, and these names can be misleading. The terminology used here is of two Villanovan phases of the ninth and eighth centuries BC, followed by the Etruscans of the Orientalizing and Archaic periods, dating approximately to the seventh and sixth centuries BC respectively. But it is also possible to call these periods Archaic I–IV, stressing the continuity, as has been done by Pallottino and other scholars.

Such differing terminologies remind us of the fragility of the evidence concerning the origin of the Etruscans. The most constructive approach is to trace the gradual growth of the community living in northern Lazio and Tuscany down these centuries. It is important to remember that the formation of a community depends not only upon the race or place of origin of its members but also on the many influences, either social, cultural, political or economic, to which they were subjected throughout their development.

This background may partly be deduced from the archaeological material that has come to light, but the student must also consider the historical and linguistic evidence, as far as it is known to us. For it is only by constant reassessment of all this evidence that we may finally be able to resolve the problem whether the Etruscans were native to Italy or what truth, if any, lies behind the story of an Etruscan migration from the east Mediterranean, the so-called 'oriental' origin of the

Etruscans, which must interest us for its historical significance and stimulate our imaginations (4).

Let us begin a review of the arguments which support these two rival theories by considering some of the references found in the ancient sources and the evidence of the language. The historians of classical times were fond of relating good stories to explain the origins of cities and peoples, often giving them an etymological flavour. In this case the most important testimony is that of Herodotus, who was writing in the fifth century BC. He recounted the following tale, which, as he mentions, was told by the Lydians themselves† :

> In the reign of Atys, the son of Manes, there was a great scarcity (of food) through the whole land of Lydia. . . . In this way they passed eighteen years. Still the affliction continued and even became more grievous. So the king determined to divide the nation in half, and to make the two portions draw lots, the one to stay, the other to leave the land. He would continue to reign over those whose lot it should be to remain behind; the emigrants should have his son Tyrrhenus for their leader. The lot was cast, and those who had to emigrate went down to Izmir, and built themselves ships, in which, after they had put aboard all needful stores, they sailed away in search of new homes and a better sustenance. After sailing past many countries they came to Umbria, where they built cities for themselves, and fixed their residence. Their former name of Lydians they laid aside, and called themselves after the name of the king's son, who led the colony, Tyrrhenians.

Hellanicus of Lesbos, writing about the same time as Herodotus, mentioned the story of a group of Pelasgians, who arrived in Italy and there changed their name to Tyrrhenians.† Confusion between Pelasgians and Tyrrhenians is interwoven in many references to the Etruscans. Some of these references are obscure or contradictory, but behind them lies a memory of the Pelasgians as a non-Greek-speaking people, who were once widely settled around the shores of the Aegean, and who, with the Tyrrhenians, had some special connection with the island of Lemnos.

These authorities accepted the story of an Etruscan migration from the east to Italy in the distant past. In Herodotus' account, the date should be placed somewhere near to that of the Trojan War, during the time of turbulence in the east Mediterranean area, when the Mycenaean civilization collapsed and the Hittite Empire fell, or in absolute dates, during the thirteenth century BC or somewhat later. The number of subsequent Greek and Roman authors who accepted the story is formidable, and some add interesting variants and embellishments. Indeed, Seneca summed up the general opinion of antiquity when he wrote, 'Asia claims the Etruscans as her own'.† It is impossible to suggest how these stories may conform with the legendary flight to the west of the Trojan hero Aeneas, and of the founding of the Roman state. Perhaps this story, too, had some special significance for the Etruscans, as several representations of the hero have been found in Etruria, including a statuette of Aeneas, bearing his father upon his shoulders, dating to the fifth century BC, which was found at Veii.

Unfortunately we have very few clues based upon Etruscan sources. Most important is the evidence of the Etruscans' own reckoning of the *saecula*, or centuries, of their race. The Etruscans believed that every race had a set span of time to run and that they themselves had been allotted ten *saecula*, a period of unequal length, which was based upon the life-span of the longest living survivor, starting at the end of the previous *saeculum*. Several Roman writers refer to this system but vary in their calculations. The most likely interpretation seems to be that the Etruscans believed their first *saeculum* had begun sometime during the eleventh or tenth century BC.

No one, perhaps not even the Etruscans themselves, appears seriously to have doubted the story of a migration from the east until the first century BC when Dionysius of Halicarnassus wrote his history with the intention of showing that the Romans, then masters of the Mediterranean world, had a Greek ancestry. He concluded that the Etruscans were an indigenous Italian race, but his arguments will not bear much scrutiny.†

To these ancient theories may be added a modern suggestion, that the Etruscans migrated from the north. This hypothesis was strongly supported during the last century and was principally based upon linguistic evidence, for some inscriptions written in an Etruscan dialect had been found among the Rhaetian Alps in the region of the upper Adige. However, it has now been pointed out that these inscriptions date from the fourth century BC or later and could be explained if some Etruscan-speaking people withdrew from the Po Valley into the mountains at the time of the Gaulish invasions, a theory suggested by Livy and other authors.† The most recent hypothesis supporting a northern origin comes from those scholars who identify the Etruscans with their predecessors, the Villanovans, and who believe the Villanovan Culture started in the region around Bologna. According to this theory, the language would have been brought south over the Apennines along with the other cultural traits of the Villanovans and the Etruscan dialect spoken in the Rhaetian Alps would indicate an even earlier area of dispersion.

Outside Italy, the only language known to have been closely similar to Etruscan is found written in inscriptions, dating to the seventh and sixth centuries BC. on the Aegean island of Lemnos, which the Greeks particularly associated with the Tyrrhenians.† For all those who believe there was an eastern element in the Etruscan people, this evidence affirms a relationship between the Etruscan language and some of the early dialects of the Aegean area. On the other hand, those who think the Etruscans were an indigenous Italian race suggest that the early dialect of Lemnos and Etruscan were scattered survivals of a language once widely spoken around the Mediterranean before the arrival of the Greeks and those Italic peoples who used the Indo-European family of languages. Both these alternatives, the arrival of an incoming language in west central Italy or the survival of an ancient tongue, could fit the pattern of linguistic regions of Italy described previously.

Can the archaeological evidence enlighten these conflicting possibilities? Some scholars, noting the quickening changes which took place in northern Lazio and Tuscany from the eighth century BC onwards, believe that these may be taken as evidence for the arrival of a new and dominant minority, the Etruscans, who were able to impose themselves as a ruling class upon the indigenous Villanovans. Many strands have been woven into this theory: the growing preference for inhumation as against cremation as their funerary rite; the similarity of some Etruscan tombs with others in the east, especially those of the royal house of Lydia; the position held by women in society and the tradition of recording the mother's as well as the father's name on funerary inscriptions, which might be related to Lycian custom.† Other evidence for this theory is seen in the forms of divination, or the interpretation of the will of the gods, used by the Etruscans and particularly of haruspicy (the examination of the livers of sacrificed animals), a form which was well known to the Babylonians and other oriental peoples, and even in the similarities of dress and artistic styles of the sixth century BC. Last but not least, it is principally the number and impact of the goods imported from the Aegean and east Mediterranean which have persuaded some scholars of the reality of an Etruscan migration from the east during the colonizing age.

Two points should be noted here. It is necessary to demonstrate a single source, and a moment in time, when a migration or migrations might have taken place, before any theory can carry conviction. Secondly, we know that the Greeks were trading along the west coast of Italy from early in the eighth century BC and that the Phoenicians may have been sailing in the west Mediterranean even before that date. Therefore we must be certain, before proposing any subsequent movement of peoples, that these trading contacts were insufficient to explain the elements from the eastern Mediterranean which appear in Etruria. We must allow for the subtle influences of such contacts, allied to the great purchasing power of the inhabitants, bringing a new wealth, the emergence of a princely class and rapid changes of taste.

With these points in mind, we may re-examine the archaeological evidence and apply new evidence which has come to light in the last decade concerning the withdrawal of Mycenaean contacts and the sequence of events during the eighth century BC. As more information becomes available about the local centres of culture in the eighth and seventh centuries BC, the clearer it becomes that a strong continuity runs from Villanovan I, through Villanovan II, when foreign goods were being imported from the east Mediterranean and Greece, into the full crescendo of the Orientalizing period, when we have evidence for Etruscans in Etruria.

The change of funerary practice was not abrupt and could spring from the re-emergence of an old Italic form; the elaboration of the tomb types may be seen as a gradual progress, partly dependent upon the new funerary rites and partly upon the new wealth, both in spending power and in ideas. The social position of women is a definite anomaly among the Italic communities, but we cannot tell when this social convention nor the practice of haruspicy reached Italy. The similarities noted from the sixth century BC have a far more compelling explanation. Above all, it is the study of the types of object imported during the eighth and seventh centuries BC which eloquently demonstrate that trade, not migration, caused the changes and started a new era.

Some Greek and east Mediterranean goods had begun to appear in northern Lazio early in the eighth century BC. In all probability these objects had been traded by the Euboean Greeks, who had established themselves on Ischia before the middle of the century. There was a gradual increase in the number of these imports, which showed a widening range and complexity of influence throughout the remainder of the Villanovan II period and on into the true Orientalizing period of the seventh century BC.

At first, local Villanovan products were hardly affected but, as time went on, more foreign forms were copied by the local craftsmen. By about the beginning of the seventh century BC, we may detect the work of immigrant Greek potters working in Etruria and, somewhat later, even suspect the presence of refugee craftsmen from the east Mediterranean, particularly from those areas affected by the expansion of Assyrian power. By this time, the west Phoenicians, and especially those of Sardinia, must have been expanding their trade. All these elements reflect the growing wealth of Etruria, which is also demonstrated by the new magnificence of the imports.

A study of these imported goods shows the intricacy of this trade. They stem from several areas of high culture in the east Mediterranean area. Moreover, many of the actual imports to Etruria from the east Mediterranean lands must have passed through Greek hands, whilst others were either adapted or copied by the Greeks, before continuing on their journey to the west. Nevertheless, it is safe to say that among the whole wide range of imported objects there is no significant group which shows a simple east to west movement. Therefore, the incoming elements demonstrate collectively, not a migration from the east, but a highly complicated development of trade which lasted for over a century.

Several types of object show the pattern of this trade but it is especially indicative to try to follow the links shown by the

6A *Horse-bit from Palestrina.*
  B *Stand from Vetulonia*

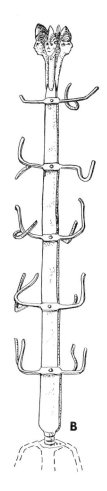

bronzes, which sometimes travelled amazing distances. There are some actual imports besides the local imitations of these foreign goods. A new form of horse-bit appears quite early in Villanovan II, with the bronze cheek-piece cast in the form of a

7 *Bronze wheeled-stand from Bisenzio in the Villa Giulia Museum, Rome*

8 *Conical stand from the Regolini-Galassi Tomb, Cerveteri, in the Vatican Museum, Rome*

horse (*6A*). The idea behind this design was probably ultimately derived from horse-gear known in Iran but the style soon mingled with Greek geometric styles in Etruria. The form of helmet worn by heads fixed to a bronze stand, found at Vetulonia and dating to the seventh century BC, are most close in form to helmets from Urartu, the Iron Age kingdom situated in the area of modern Armenia (*6B*). An extraordinary wheeled-stand from Bisenzio is a local copy, made early in the seventh century BC, of a type best known in the Cypriot Late Bronze Age, whence it passed to Crete and, in all likelihood, on to Italy (*7*).

Two high conical stands, used to support cauldrons, from Palestrina are imports from the east, but it is probable that the associated cauldrons were made in Greece. These were copies of an eastern type, and, in their turn, the Etruscans imitated the form, as may be seen from an example found in the Regolini-Galassi Tomb (*8*). Among the other actual imports from the east during this period are the silver bowls from a Phoenician source; a bronze head of a lion of Assyrian manufacture from Veii; and a trident found at Vetulonia, for which the closest analogies come from the Caucasian or Iranian region. Finally, a bronze cauldron with attachments modelled as the heads of bulls from Cuma and a *fibula* from southern Lazio show that Phrygia and western Asia Minor were not entirely without contact with the west, though imports from this area are conspicuously lacking from Etruria.

All these objects demonstrate the wide divergence of origin of the imported goods, which began to mingle with local forms quite early in the eighth century BC. It is clear that they represent a trading relationship similar to that established at a slightly earlier date between Greece and the east Mediterranean, which led to a revolution in taste, as it did in Etruria.

If this interpretation is correct, is it still possible to reconcile the strong tradition of an Etruscan migration from the east with archaeological evidence? Working backwards from the time of the first written sources of the seventh century BC, we have found no sign of a migration, either then or during the preceding Villanovan II period, which began about 800 BC. We should thus be prepared to identify the Etruscans with their predecessors in our region. This early presence of Etruscans in the west fits with Ephorus' comment that before the Greeks founded colonies in Sicily, that is, before 734 BC, Greek sailors were terrorized by Tyrrhenian pirates in the western seas. Also, if we may rely upon the early date for the passage, it accords with Hesiod's reference to Tyrrhenians in the west.†

There is no break in the continuity between Villanovan II and Villanovan I of the ninth century BC. At present there is also no evidence of a significant movement of people in northern Lazio or Tuscany during this period, nor do we know of direct trade with the Aegean or east Mediterranean. Yet there are traces of east Mediterranean traditions in the cultures of west central Italy at this time and, even earlier, there are a few actual imported objects from the east Mediterranean area. Among them are fragments of a bronze tripod, which would be datable in a Cypriot context to the twelfth or early eleventh century BC, and which were found in an Umbrian context of the late tenth century BC.

The tenuous and indirect links possibly established by the Phoenicians in the west Mediterranean about this time might explain such phenomena. But it seems more likely that both the actual imports and the traditions from the east Mediterranean discernible during the Villanovan I period were relics, either from the time when Mycenaean sailors were still active in the west or from the subsequent period, during which some influences may have reached Italy from the east by sea. These tantalizing glimpses into what was already the remote past at the time our written records begin, are too inconclusive for us to accept them as sure evidence of a migration from the east at an early date. Nevertheless, they are sufficient to ensure that the question should remain open and to turn our imagination to the legend of Tyrrhenus.

3

The history of Etruria to the end of the Roman republic

The centuries of Etruscan power and prosperity run parallel with the Orientalizing, Archaic, Classical and Hellenistic periods of Greece and the rise of the Republic of Rome. This is one of the attractions of studying the Etruscans, since their history may be seen against a background both of the great events and artistic achievements of the Mediterranean civilizations and the gradual diffusion of influences from these cultures to the barbarian peoples of Italy and Europe.

Since we have very few Etruscan records, little is known of the internal history of Etruria. In the artistic field, however, it is becoming possible to trace some of the varying relationships between the cities and with the world outside Etruria. We can only follow the fortunes of the Etruscans through references made by Greek and Roman authors, sometimes written in the spirit of rivalry and often long after the events they describe. Moreover, the principal interest of Greek and Roman historians was concentrated elsewhere and we frequently have to deduce the conditions of Etruria from events which took place abroad. Nevertheless, it is possible to trace in outline the early development of Etruria and to follow the struggle for power with Rome. The best record was made by Livy, who was writing in the first century BC, when it was already becoming difficult to imagine the Etruscans at the height of their prestige.

The Etruscans were entering the so-called Orientalizing period early in the seventh century BC. The moment taken to mark the beginning of this period may be roundly placed at 700 BC or at the time of the Bocchoris Tomb at Tarquinia, dated about 675 BC, whose contents included objects in the Villanovan tradition, as well as imports and local goods, showing the influence of Greece and the east Mediterranean. During the eighth century, the incoming elements had been mainly concentrated at sites in northern Lazio, closely linked by land and sea with Campania, but now graves of equal wealth and with imported goods begin to appear at Vetulonia, Populonia and other sites in the metal-bearing zone along the north coast. Gradually, these new styles spread across the whole region.

With this diffusion, Etruria was finally drawn out of the European sphere and took her place as a Mediterranean civilization, herself passing the Orientalizing forms to her neighbours, who, in their turn, influenced the adjacent peoples. Thus it was that the tide of trade, which had for so long flowed south, now began to turn and styles from Italy reached northwards into Europe beyond the Alps.

Both Greeks and Phoenicians continued to expand their colonial grasp in the west Mediterranean, sometimes with particular consequences for the Etruscans. The Phoenicians had settled on the south and west coasts of Sardinia and begun their long struggle to dominate the whole island. A group of Chalcidian Greeks from Cuma founded a colony at Messina (Zankle), on the Sicilian side of the Straits of Messina. This foundation was soon balanced by another at Reggio (Rhegium) on the opposite shore, thus placing this sea road effectively in the hands of the Greeks. The Greek city of Sybaris, on the west coast of the Gulf of Taranto, placed daughter colonies at Paestum (Poseidonia) and near the River Lao (Laos), across the narrow isthmus at the north of Calabria, which gave her access overland to the Tyrrhenian Sea.

Trade, based upon the exploitation of her great mineral resources, brought a new wealth to Etruria during the seventh century BC. Meanwhile, other inter-related developments were taking place. The groups of Villanovan villages were beginning to cohere into towns and, with their increasing control of the surrounding districts, perhaps the nucleus of a city-state was already forming. The new princely class built fine family tombs and we know that Etruria was even able to attract a distinguished migrant to her shores. A Greek nobleman, Demaratus of Corinth, left his native city at a moment of political crisis in the middle of the seventh century and, bringing Greek artists with him, he settled at Tarquinia.†

We are told that Demaratus had two sons and one, called Lucumo in the Roman sources, married a high-born Etruscan lady, Tanaquil. Lucumo could not advance himself at Tarquinia, as he was not of pure Etruscan blood, and, urged by his wife who could not stand the indignity, he left Tarquinia for Rome. Livy writes †:

> They had come, as it happened, as far as the Janiculum, when as they were sitting in their covered wagon (*carpentum*), an eagle poised on its wings gently descended upon them and plucked off Lucumo's cap, after which, rising noisily above the car and again stooping, as if sent from heaven for that service, it deftly replaced the cap upon his head and departed on high. This augury was joyfully accepted, it is said, by Tanaquil, a woman skilled in celestial prodigies, as was the case with most Etruscans.

She then interpreted the omen and told Lucumo to expect greatness, and her prophecy was fulfilled when he became the first Etruscan king of Rome, taking the name of Lucius Tarquinius. As king, he fought with the Sabines, struggled to enlarge Rome's power among the Latin peoples, and is said to have undertaken building works in the city.

He was succeeded by Servius Tullius, about whom many stories are told. The Emperor Claudius was deeply learned in Etruscan history and parts of a speech have been preserved in which he mentioned that Servius Tullius was called Macstarna by the Etruscans and that he was a constant companion of Caelius Vibenna in all his adventures.† We know of this Caelius Vibenna and of his brother, Aulus, both from Etruscan epigraphic evidence, Roman sources and several Etruscan illustrations of their exploits. Most famous are the scenes on the walls of the François Tomb at Vulci, their native city, which were probably painted during the second or early first century BC (*51*). The painting shows a struggle between several pairs of combatants, identified by the names written beside them. The painting presents a legend told of those days when the city-states and, perhaps, the rival captains of troops warred among themselves. It may well be a truthful illustration of the conditions prevailing in Etruria during the early part of the sixth century BC.

The traditional dates for the reign of Lucius Tarquinius the

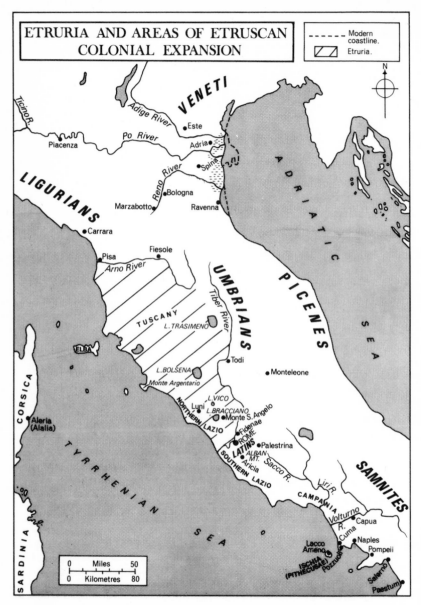

9 Map of Etruria and areas of Etruscan colonial expansion

Elder at Rome are 616–578 BC. It can hardly be considered a coincidence that, about 600 BC, the Etruscans were able to advance southwards into the rich plain of Campania, where for the first time their power encroached upon that of the Greeks of Cuma. Their proximity proved most fruitful in cultural exchange throughout the sixth century (9). It is not clear just what form this colonial expansion took. To correspond with the twelve cities of Etruria, twelve colonies are said to have been founded, the greatest of which was ancient Capua (modern Santa Maria di Capua Vetere), which the Etruscans called Volturnum, a name still retained by the river close by.† By-passing Cuma by an inland route, the Etruscans may even have advanced south of Salerno and thus established contact with Paestum (Poseidonia) and thence with Sybaris, her mother city, which was at this time enjoying great wealth.† Sybaris was famous for her close ties with Miletus, a Greek city in Asia Minor, and this, no doubt, was a main route by which Ionian styles reached Etruria and profoundly affected the taste of the period. There is also evidence for Ionian artists working in Etruria, presumably refugees from the crisis of the second half of the sixth century when the Greek cities of Asia Minor had to submit to Lydia and, after her defeat in 546 BC, also became part of the Persian Empire.

By about 525 BC the Etruscans had also expanded over the low passes of the Apennines into the district around Bologna, which had for long been a great centre of the north Villanovan Culture. A tradition said that the Etruscan city there, called Felsina, was founded by Ocnus, the son or brother of the founder of Perugia.† We may guess that the northern cities, especially Volterra, were involved in this colonization. Twelve cities were said to have been founded, but we do not know the exact limits of the advance. The archaeological record suggests that the Etruscans did not reach beyond the western borders of Emilia. To the north of the Po, traces of the Etruscans are few, and it is very doubtful if they ever settled west of the River Ticino, near whose banks the first great battle with the Gauls was fought. Indeed, we may be confident that Livy gave an exaggerated account when he said the Etruscans held the whole valley up to the foothills of the Alps, except for the land of the Veneti in the area around modern Venice. At this time the

Etruscans reached the height of their confident expansion and came closest to fulfilling the description given by Cato that 'nearly all Italy had been under the domination of the Etruscans'.†

The two ports of Spina and Adria gave the north Etruscans access to the Adriatic Sea. We may trace the growth in prosperity and an important trading contact of the Etruscan settlements in the lower Po Valley by the number of vases imported from Attica. In the late sixth and early fifth centuries BC, these imports reached a high figure and it is clear that the Adriatic offered an outlet to the east when the Etruscan relationship with the Greeks in the Tyrrhenian Sea was becoming increasingly hostile.

The seeds of this hostility had been growing with the clash of interests in Campania but the rivalry between the Etruscans and Greeks at sea was already old, and now reached a crisis in the struggle for naval supremacy. The Phocaeans, from a Greek city of outstanding naval ability in Asia Minor, defeated the Carthaginians at sea and founded a colony at Marseille, on the mouth of the Rhône, about 600 BC. Some forty years later they placed a colony at Alalia (modern Aleria) on the east coast of Corsica and it is possible that they also tried to settle in Sardinia. After the fall of Lydia in 546 BC, the cities of Ionia were threatened by the Persians and a proposal was made at the Panionian Conference that the Greeks of Asia Minor should migrate in a body to Sardinia. This plan was never carried out but nearly half the citizens of Phocaea did join the colony at Alalia. Greek colonization of the Corsican coast opposite Etruria must have alarmed the coastal cities. Moreover, the Carthaginians, who had now assumed an imperial rôle among the Phoenicians of the west, were equally intolerant of any encroachment upon Sardinia. At this time the Etruscans and Carthaginians were working in close alliance, so close that Aristotle later quoted them as an example of allied states.†

About 535 BC the combined fleets of the Etruscans and Carthaginians met the Phocaeans in battle. The Phocaeans won a narrow victory but lost so many ships that they had to abandon Alalia and finally settled at Velia, south of Paestum. Sardinia remained in the hands of the Carthaginians and the Etruscans founded a colony on Corsica. Herodotus tells us that after the battle the Carthaginians and Etruscans took their prisoners ashore and stoned them to death. Afterwards a sickness began to afflict those who passed by the place and the people of Cerveteri (Caere) sent a deputation to Delphi to ask how they might atone for their sin. The oracle told them to institute funerary games in honour of the dead and, when this was done, the plague ceased. Herodotus adds that the games were still celebrated in his own day.†

About ten years later, in 524 BC, the Etruscans again met the Greeks in battle, this time on land and with the domination of Campania at stake. We are told that the Etruscans tried to take Cuma and assembled an army of half a million men but that Aristodemos of Cuma defeated them with a fraction the number of troops, himself killing the enemy general in single combat.† Another event took place in 510 BC, which was to affect the Etruscans deeply. The Greek city of Sybaris had long been a rival of the neighbouring city of Croton and, in this year, the Crotoniates completely defeated her; the city was razed to the ground and the inhabitants fled. The Greeks of the Straits of Messina controlled the remaining route to the east by sea and behind them was the growing power of Syracuse.

Almost simultaneously the Etruscans suffered another reverse. Tarquinius Superbus, the Proud, had succeeded Servius Tullius as king of Rome and is credited with enhancing Rome's power among her Latin neighbours and organizing several magnificent public building works in the city. However, his arrogance, with that of his wife and sons, lost him the support of the aristocracy and people. A revolution took place, expelling the last Etruscan king of Rome and establishing a Republic, traditionally in 509 BC. Subsequent events are confused. Tradition recounted that the Tarquins asked help of Lars Porsenna, king of Clusium (modern Chiusi) and that he besieged Rome, though it is not clear with what success. Few occasions in early Roman history gathered more stories and, we may suspect, gave occasion for some rousing Roman propaganda.†

Whatever may remain in doubt, it is certain that Porsenna retired without re-establishing the Tarquins at Rome. A little later we hear of an Etruscan defeat near Aricia, a town lying to the south of Rome. Subsequently the Etruscans withdrew and thus recognized the loss of their leadership in southern Lazio and of the routes leading south into Campania.†

We have seen that the Greek cities of Asia Minor had been incorporated into the Persian Empire in 545 BC. At the turn of the century they revolted, the cities of the Greek mainland became involved, and the fifth century opened with the great struggle between Greeks and Persians. This was resolved by the Greek victories at Salamis in 480 BC and Plataea. It was said in antiquity that, on the same day as the battle of Salamis, the Sicilian Greeks won a decisive battle against the barbarians of the west.† The end of the sixth century had, indeed, seen a growing tension between the Greeks and Carthaginians and, in 480 BC, the latter sent a huge expeditionary force to Sicily. They were opposed by the Greek cities under the leadership of Syracuse, which won a great victory at Himera. This battle decided that for the next eighty years the Greeks, and especially Syracuse, should play a dominant rôle in Sicily.† The continued close association between the Etruscans and Carthaginians at this time has recently been demonstrated by the discovery of three gold plaques at Pyrgi, one of the ports of Cerveteri (Caere). These plaques were inscribed; one was written in Punic script while the others were translated into Etruscan.

A major defeat of her allies could not fail to have adverse repercussions for the Etruscans, nor were these long in coming. The Etruscans of Campania were now dependent upon support by sea. In 474 BC, the Greeks of Cuma asked help from Syracuse and Hieron sent his fleet into the Tyrrhenian Sea and there defeated the Etruscans off Cuma. After the battle, a captured Etruscan helmet was inscribed and Hieron dedicated it at Olympia. It was found there in 1817 and is now in the British Museum (10). Hieron followed his victory by placing a garrison on Ischia and, later in the century, we hear of Syracusan raids on Elba and the Etruscan settlements of Corsica.†

The Etruscans had lost their former supremacy in the Tyrrhenian Sea and, during the fifth century, it also became apparent who were to become their greatest opponents on land. The young Roman Republic was gathering strength; she gained the leadership of her Latin neighbours and fought with the hill tribes. A somewhat similar situation occurred in Campania, where the peoples of the Samnite hills swept down

10 Bronze Etruscan helmet, dedicated at Olympia by Hieron of Syracuse. In the British Museum

to the plain and captured Capua in 423 BC, thus breaking Etruscan power in the region, and soon also took Greek Cuma.

The fifth century and first half of the fourth century BC saw the first phase of the long struggle between the Etruscan states and Rome. It began with a series of campaigns centering on Fidenae (modern Fidene), a small town allied with the Etruscans, which lay on the left bank of the Tiber only ten kilometres (six miles) upstream of Rome. Fidenae was taken at last by the Romans in 435 BC and, in the following years, there was almost annual war with Veii, the great Etruscan city which lay only eighteen kilometres (eleven miles) to the north of Rome.

In this crisis the Veientes joined with their neighbours and allies the Faliscans, a people who inhabited an area around Civita Castellana on the right bank of the Tiber and who accepted Etruscan culture though they spoke a dialect akin to Latin. Both peoples realized their danger and the first formal attempts to unite the Etruscan city-states in common action are recorded at this time. The Etruscans, however, did not act together, some because of their dislike of the newly chosen king of Veii and others pleading the pressure of the Gauls from the north.† Thus Veii was left to face the Romans alone but for the help of the Faliscans.

In 405 BC the epic ten-year siege of Veii began. Many stories were told about it in the days when Rome ruled the Mediterranean world. But there was also a clear contemporary realization of what was at stake, judging from the new and severe war measures imposed at Rome. Livy gives a tremendous account of these years, of the building of entrenchments around Veii, manned through the winter months, of the harassment of the blockading troops by the Faliscans and of retaliatory attacks upon Capena and Falerii (modern Civita Castellana). Throughout the account there runs a constant Roman fear that the city-states of Etruria might combine against them. In 396 BC the Romans took Veii. They sacked the city, sold the inhabitants into slavery, and incorporated her territory into that of Rome, whose victory was complete and permanent.†

The fall of Veii was a grave disaster for the Etruscans since it breached their natural frontier to the south. Yet this frontier remained intact until the Etruscans were attacked by a scarcely less formidable, though less consistent, foe from the north. Gaulish tribes from north of the Alps were infiltrating into the Po Valley by the fifth century BC, bringing with them an off-shoot of the *La Tène* Culture, the name given to the second great period of the European Iron Age. In Italy, they both influenced the neighbouring peoples and learned from them. Gauls begin to appear in Etruscan art towards the end of the fifth century, often in battle scenes like that on a *stele* at Bologna (*84*). By this time they must have begun to harass the northern settlements and we hear of an Etruscan city, which fell at the same time as Veii. The archaeological record at Marzabotto and Bologna shows that the Etruscans were ousted quite early in the fourth century BC and the Gauls settled widely in the Po Valley, so that the Romans later called it Cisalpine Gaul.†

For a time the Adriatic ports continued to import Greek goods, a trade no doubt welcomed by the Gauls, and about this time we hear of a new interest of Syracuse in the Adriatic. The old emnity between the Etruscans and Syracuse had continued in 413 BC when the former sent three ships to help the Athenians at the siege of Syracuse during the Peloponnesian War. Then, perhaps, Dionysius of Syracuse took advantage of Etruscan weakness in the north to enlarge his Adriatic Empire by domination of Adria and Spina. His hostility in the Tyrrhenian Sea is well attested, since his fleets raided the coasts of Corsica and Etruria and sacked the sanctuary of Pyrgi in 384 BC.†

The Gauls did not long remain confined to the Po Valley. In 391 BC they crossed the Apennines. The story of Arruns of Clusium (modern Chiusi) may relate to this time; it was said that he had enticed the Gauls across the Alps by gifts of fruits and especially of wine, in order to avenge a private quarrel. His wife had been seduced by a noble, called Lucumo by Livy, and 'this youth, whose guardian he had been, was so powerful that he could not have chastised him without calling in a foreign force'.†

Faced with a Gaulish invasion, the people of Chiusi asked help of Rome. The Romans, perhaps in anticipation of their own defence, sent ambassadors, who, instead of being conciliatory, joined the Etruscan battle-line in the ensuing struggle near Chiusi. In retaliation, the Gauls marched on Rome. They defeated a Roman army near the Allia, a small tributary of the Tiber, and captured and burned the city, with the exception of the Capitol, though they did not occupy it for long.† In this crisis, the people of Caere (modern Cerveteri) showed sympathy with the Romans, giving asylum to their priests, Vestals and sacred objects. In later years, the Romans remembered this act of friendship.

Though their defeat at the Allia had momentarily discredited the Romans, the southern Etruscan cities and the Faliscans were soon again under pressure. Following the seizure of the territory of Veii, the Romans subdued Faliscan Capena and effectively advanced her new frontier as far north as Monte Soratte on the right bank of the Tiber, encroaching upon the territory of the Faliscan city at Civita Castellana (Falerii Veteres). To the west, the frontier ran along the foothills of the Ciminian range, passing Sutri (Sutrium) and Nepi (Nepete), both admirably situated as garrisons guarding the routes north and westward into the territory of the great Etruscan city of Tarquinia. During the first half of the fourth century BC, Cerveteri (Caere), Civita Castellana (Falerii Veteres) and Tarquinia were all involved in hostilities with Rome. Between 358 and 351 BC, war was practically continuous and a bitter campaign was fought between Rome and Tarquinia. In 353 BC Cerveteri was granted a truce for one hundred years and may even have gained a form of Roman citizenship. Tarquinia and Civita Castellana sued for peace in 351 BC and were given truces for forty years, though shortly afterwards the latter became a subject-ally of Rome. Thus the weight of Roman power was spreading over southern Etruria.

The peace was observed for the whole forty years. During this time Alexander led his army to the east, and it is recorded that the Etruscans were among the Mediterranean peoples who sent an embassy to greet him on his return to Babylon.†
In Italy, war broke out between Rome and the Samnites but, presumably restrained by their truces, the Etruscan states took no advantage to harass the Romans from the north until the truce ran out. Then, in 311 BC, war was resumed, and the next half century saw the second and final phase of the struggle with Rome, which ended in the extinction of the Etruscan city-states as independent political entities. This was only part of the spread of Roman power over much of the Italian peninsula at this time and should be compared with the growing Roman domination of the Samnites, Umbrians and other peoples of Italy.

In 311 BC most of the Etruscan cities did combine and assembled at Sutri (Sutrium) to besiege the town and a bitterly contested battle ensued. A repetition of events followed the next year but on this occasion the Etruscans were defeated, some fleeing into the forest, which still covered the Ciminian range. The Roman Consul wished to pursue them but few Romans were brave enough to venture into the forest. Since he could speak Etruscan, the Consul's brother offered to reconnoitre the area and, on his safe return, the Consul set out with the army, marched to the top of the Ciminian range and saw below them the rich lands of Etruria. Though the details are obscure, it is clear that in this campaign the Romans did advance into the upper Tiber basin and, after a struggle, the great Etruscan cities of that region, Perugia (Perusia), Cortona and Arezzo (Arretium) sued for peace and were given truces for thirty years; in 308 BC Tarquinia began another forty-year truce.†

A short peace followed but soon afterwards widespread hostilities recurred in the north, with the Romans involved in the affairs of Arezzo (Arretium) and of battles near Roselle (Rusellae) and Volterra (Volaterrae). In 299 BC, a Gaulish raid into Roman territory was supported by Etruscans. Then the Samnites, who had been defeated in their great confrontation with Rome, marched north and created a coalition of Umbrians, Gauls and Etruscans. The latter, however, appear to have played a minor part in the following campaign, which ended in a decisive Roman victory at Sentinum in Umbria in 295 BC. A final struggle developed. Roselle was taken, Bolsena was attacked and defeated, there was a Roman victory over Vulci and further truces with Perugia (Perusia) and Arezzo (Arretium). In 282 BC an alliance of Gauls and Etruscans was overcome at Lake Vadimo. By 280 BC, when the Romans turned to face the landing of Pyrrhus of Epirus in the south of Italy, a general settlement of Etruria appears to have been reached.†

We know of two important incidents during the third century BC. In 265 BC, there was a revolutionary uprising in Bolsena (Volsinii) and the ruling families asked help of Rome (p. 167). The latter restored order and moved the city from its easily defended position down to the shores of the lake. Roman ascendancy was symbolized by the removal to Rome of the cult of the Etruscan god, Voltumna (Vertumnus or Vortumnus). A similar fate overtook the people of Civita Castellana (Falerii Veteres), when they revolted in 241 BC and the inhabitants were removed from their precipitous city site to one in open country.

By this time the Romans had fought and emerged victorious from the First Punic War. Their power was consolidated in the south of the peninsula, while the Carthaginians finally abandoned all claims in Sicily. Shortly afterwards, Rome also acquired Sardinia and Corsica. After these events, there could be no doubt of the Roman supremacy in Italy and, in Etruria as elsewhere, this was emphasized by the settling of colonies in strategic places and by the building of the great Roman military highways (p. 142).

With the exception of Cerveteri (Caere), which may have gained a form of Roman citizenship at an early date, the Etruscan cities continued to live as Roman allies under individual treaties. They were allowed no political dealings with other states and owed Rome military service and, it seems, their people had no right to own property in Roman territory nor to marry Roman citizens. Yet these restrictions must have been lightly applied and tolerable as the Romans were able to rely upon the Etruscans in the last great Gaulish raid into Etruria in 225 BC, when the Gauls were decisively defeated near

Talamone. In the years immediately following this victory the Romans went on to conquer the Gaulish tribes living in the Po Valley. Moreover, no Etruscan city revolted during the Second Punic War, when Hannibal and his Carthaginian army invaded Italy and for long the outcome of this great struggle remained in doubt.

The Etruscan cities and people did not immediately lose their individual character with the demise of their political independence. Local artistic forms continued throughout the second and into the first century BC and it is convenient to call this period Romano-Etruscan or Etruscan of the Hellenistic period, as is generally done in this book. Nevertheless, during this time the Etruscans were gradually becoming absorbed into the way of life of the Romans, whose power now stretched around the Mediterranean. The interest of historians had moved away from Etruria and we know very few details of local affairs during the second century BC. As in the rest of Italy, however, there were severe social and economic effects from the Second Punic War and we hear of a slave revolt in 196 BC and of agricultural depression.

At the beginning of the first century BC, the Social War was fought between Romans and a confederation of rebellious Italian peoples, including the Etruscans and, in 89 BC, they were given the Roman citizenship. Later in the century, Etruria suffered considerably in the vicious discords of the Late Roman Republic. Peace was finally restored by Augustus, who, believing that the old political system of the Republic could no longer provide an effective government, established an authoritarian regime and the Imperial period began.

By now, the process of assimilation of the Etruscan cities was almost complete. Augustus's great minister, Maecenas, was proud of his princely Etruscan ancestry; men of Etruscan descent and Roman scholars interested themselves in Etruscan antiquities, while contemporary Etruscan inscriptions become few in number and the art merges into the style of Imperial Rome. Yet we may suppose that in the second century AD some rustic people of Etruria still spoke the language.† The traditional knowledge of the diviners lasted even longer. Julian the Apostate took Etruscan haruspices with him on his march into Asia in the fourth century AD and another haruspex offered to enlist the lightning to drive Alaric from the walls of Rome in AD 410.

This outline of the history of Etruria has illustrated some points which are essential in assessing the life of the Etruscans down the centuries. Their most glorious period was during the Archaic Age, when historical references are few and we may only draw a fuller picture in the period of their decline; and for this we must mainly rely upon the records of their enemies. It was the misfortune of the Etruscans to be the rivals of the Greeks at sea during the height of their power and to be the military opponents of the Romans and Gauls, both most formidable in war. The Etruscans, however, failed to unite their cities when need arose and they did not resolve the division between the classes. While Rome assimilated first her Latin neighbours and then peoples far less closely allied to her in culture, and adapted her constitution to the gradual erosion of exclusive hereditary privileges, the Etruscan cities maintained their traditional attitudes and paid a high penalty for it.

4

The cities and their tombs

The beauty of the landscape in Etruria has been celebrated down the centuries and the modern traveller, in search of Etruscan places, will find delight not only in the evocative ruins left by the Etruscans but also in the monuments of the Roman, Medieval and Renaissance eras. At some places, where a city was sacked in antiquity or a population moved, ruins of the Etruscan period lie open to the eye or buried but available to the spade. At other sites, which have been continuously occupied to this day, traces of the Etruscan period have been all but obliterated or overlaid by buildings of succeeding periods.

The Etruscan cities had a remarkable individuality. The lack of centralization, so strongly reflected in their history, has bequeathed us a legacy of very differing sites with no strict uniformity of plan, tomb type or artistic expression.

Yet the cities of Etruria shared a common political function. Each was the metropolis of a city-state, as Athens was in Attica, and each spread its individual character over the territory within its control. We do not know precisely where their political boundaries lay and these no doubt altered down the centuries as the cities grew or waned in power. However, we may trace their areas of influence through the local styles of art and from such evidence as that of their road systems, linking the city with the surrounding country. We cannot suggest the exact number of inhabitants of these city-states but from an estimate based upon the known burials and the life expectancy, it has been calculated that Cerveteri (Caere) had a population of about 25,000 people at the period of its prosperity.

Let us, then, begin a brief survey of Etruria at Cerveteri (Caere), the most southerly of the great coastal cities, whose territory bordered to the south with that of Veii, with Tarquinia to the north and ran inland to Lake Bracciano (*11*). Thus it included the metal-bearing Tolfa Hills, which must explain her early prosperity and may well be the principal reason for her continued close relations with the Greeks, who called the city Agylla. She had a treasury at Delphi and the Greeks said

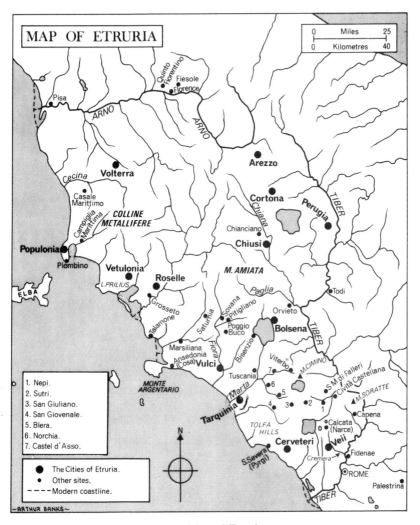

11 Map of Etruria

that Cerveteri, alone among the Etruscan states, abstained from piracy.† Certainly her fortunes were founded upon sea trade and her decline set in with the loss of Etruscan sea power.

The city lay within sight of the sea, its western end lying on a steep scarp as it rose from the coastal plain, while the valleys of two streams bounded the urban area to north and south. Low cliffs follow the rims of these valleys and, along their line, are the remains of city walls. Like several other Etruscan sites, it is the cemeteries which must chiefly claim our attention at Cerveteri. As the Villanovans before them, the Etruscans buried their dead outside the area of habitation. An early cemetery, Sorbo, lies between the city and the coastal plain and here the graves were mainly *pozzetti* and *fosse* but, among them, lay the Regolini-Galassi Tomb, discovered in 1836 and named after its two excavators (5). An earthen mound, or *tumulus*, once covered the tomb, which had a stepped entrance passage, an outer corridor flanked by a niche or cell on either side and a long, narrow inner chamber. This was partly cut into the rock but was vaulted with cut blocks of stone, forming a false vault. The tomb was unrobbed and the incredibly rich contents, dating to the Orientalizing period, belonged to a woman and two men, one of whom was cremated. These objects may now be seen in the Vatican Museum in Rome (*8, 71, 75*).

Air photography has done much to reveal the extent of the cemeteries at Cerveteri, often in areas where the tombs are no longer visible from the ground. However, the carefully excavated and restored necropolis of Banditaccia is by far the most impressive place to visit, for it is a veritable city of the dead, now charmingly planted with shrubs and cypress trees (*12, 13*). From the ancient city, a rock-cut road led north across the intervening valley and along the back of the hill on which the cemetery lies. It was the Etruscan funerary way and the surface is worn into deep ruts by the wheels of carriages as they passed in funerary processions. At the sides of this road and of the smaller alleys, branching to left and right, lie the tombs, whose characteristic forms altered down the centuries. There are the great early *tumuli*, often with several separate tombs enclosed within the perimeter wall with its moulded decoration; then, there are the neat rows of cells, built with cut blocks of stone, and the later chambers, dug deep into the rock. The visitor may wander among the tombs and explore their dark interiors.

12 Air view of the Banditaccia cemetery at Cerveteri

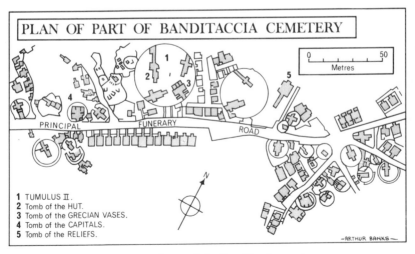

PLAN OF PART OF BANDITACCIA CEMETERY

0   50
Metres

PRINCIPAL   FUNERARY   ROAD

1 TUMULUS II.
2 Tomb of the HUT.
3 Tomb of the GRECIAN VASES.
4 Tomb of the CAPITALS.
5 Tomb of the RELIEFS.

—ARTHUR BANKS—

13 Plan of part of the Banditaccia cemetery

By the entrance to the tombs, there was often placed a group of small *cippi*, a phallic form to denote the grave of a man and a small symbol of a house for that of a woman. The people of Cerveteri (Caere) abandoned the rite of cremation quite early and placed their dead in the tombs, lying on the benches or niches, sometimes in terracotta sarcophagi (*73, 35*). With them, they buried some of their personal possessions and a representative collection of these objects may be seen in the Archaeological Museum in the town.

Near the present tower of Santa Severa lay one of Cerveteri's chief ports and the sanctuary of Pyrgi, famous in antiquity for its wealth. This site has recently been discovered and the foundations of two temples have been excavated (*26*). Magnificent temple terracottas were found and the gold plaques with a bilingual inscription, which are now in the Etruscan Museum of the Villa Giulia in Rome.

The geographical position of Veii (modern Veio near Isola Farnese), lying between the territory of Cerveteri to the west, the land of the Faliscans to the north-east and with her long southern border along the right bank of the Tiber, determined that she should soon become the rival of Rome. The whole history of Etruria hinged upon her conquest by the Romans in 396 BC. It was said that, after the subsequent sack of Rome by the Gauls, only the authority of Camillus prevented the population of Rome from moving to the almost impregnable site of Veii, so great was its prestige at that time.† This ancient glory, contrasted to a contemporary neglect, was already a theme for the reflections of the Augustan poet, Propertius, writing in the first century BC.†

> Veii, thou hadst a royal crown of old,
> And in thy forum stood a throne of gold!
> Thy walls now echo but the shepherd's horn,
> And o'er thine ashes waves the summer corn.

The city of Veii lay just to the north of Rome. The surrounding landscape is typical of the volcanic region of southern Etruria and the site is characteristic of the defensive positions so often selected for the towns and cities in this area. Both the city and its citadel, or acropolis, were surrounded by ravines, which formed so formidable a protection that no city walls were built until the threat of Rome became strong. Inside the line of the walls, excavation has revealed a scattered Villanovan occupation and, on the acropolis, this was found stratified beneath Etruscan buildings. Some houses have been dug and the position of temples has been indicated by finds of their terracotta decorations.

The most famous temple site at Veii, however, lies at the side of a ravine to the south-west of the urban area. Here, at the Portonaccio sanctuary, an enclosure wall, altar, temple foundations and water tanks have been found and it has been suggested that the cult was concerned with the healing power of the waters. The most exciting discovery was that of a group of terracotta statues from the temple, including the Apollo of Veii, found in 1916 and now in the Villa Giulia Museum in Rome. The group dates from c. 500 BC and it is interesting to recall that Varro knew of a tradition which stated that Vulca, the only Etruscan artist we know by name, was summoned from Veii to Rome during the regal period, in order to model the image of Jupiter in terracotta for the Capitoline Temple.† The Portonaccio group has, therefore, been attributed to Vulca or his school (p. 81).

The region around Veii is remarkable for the number of rock-cut passages, or *cuniculi*, designed for both the collection and regulation of water (p. 148). A *cuniculus* was driven through the hill to the west of the city, in order to carry water from one stream into the course of another, while the famed Ponte Sodo, a large irregular tunnel, some four to five metres (about fifteen feet) wide, six to eight metres (about twenty-one feet) high and over seventy-five metres (eighty-two yards) in length, was cut through a ridge of rock at the north side of the city and served both as a bridge over the bed of the stream and to divert its flood water. Rock-cut sewers are visible at many town sites in this region and it may well be that the stories of the capture of both Fidenae and Veii by means of such underground passages were based upon the observation of such tunnels, or, indeed, upon fact.

The Etruscan cemeteries at Veii are not well known but include two early painted tombs; one of these, named the Campana Tomb, was found in 1842 and was drawn by Canina, a contemporary Italian artist, with its funerary goods still in position (*14*). The tomb is cut into the hillside and, at the entrance, there stood two guardian sphinxes, carved in stone. On a bench in the outer chamber lay the skeleton of a warrior, surrounded by his possessions, whose helmet had been holed by a blow, perhaps the cause of his death.

14 Sketch by Canina of the Campana Tomb, Veii, as it was found

To the north and east of the territory of Veii lay the land of the Faliscans who were politically and culturally affiliated with the Etruscans and particularly with Veii. The largest Faliscan centre was at Civita Castellana (Falerii Veteres), lying at the edge of the Tiber Valley to the north of Monte Soratte. The city crowned a site almost completely surrounded by high cliffs, and has produced an outstanding series of temple terra-cottas (*82*). When the Romans subdued the rebellious city in 241 BC, they forced the inhabitants to move from this uniquely defensible position to Falerii Novi (modern S. Maria di Falleri), a site set in open country some six kilometres (four miles) distant. This, in its turn, was abandoned in the Middle Ages but a magnificent circuit of turreted walls and fine gateways survive.

Not far to the south-west lay two small Etruscan towns at

Nepi (Nepete) and Sutri (Sutrium); rock-cut tombs line the cliff face of the neighbouring ravines but little else remains from the period before the conquest of Veii. There is a delightful small amphitheatre at Sutri, cut from the rock, and the situation of the town, set upon a flat hill-top and surrounded by cliffs may be taken as characteristic of many south Etruscan sites. Canina caught this aspect in his imaginative reconstruction of the approach to the town, adding a paved roadway, a gate and towers (*frontispiece*).

In the fourth century BC, the Latin colonies at Sutri and Nepi guarded the 'gates of Etruria',† or the routes leading north and west into the territory of Tarquinia, the great coastal city, lying some forty kilometres (twenty-five miles) to the north of Cerveteri, whose power dominated the valley of the Marta. No city of Etruria enjoyed a higher prestige than Tarquinia (Tarquinii). Her name was connected with the brother or son of Tyrrhenus, Tarchon, who was said to have received command upon their arrival in Italy and to have founded twelve cities.† Another story told how the Etruscan laws of divination had been revealed at Tarquinia and the rise of the Tarquin family to royal power in Rome has already been related. It is clear that the heroic deeds of the past were still remembered in Roman times. Several Latin inscriptions, which describe the careers of great men of Tarquinia during the previous centuries, were found in 1948.

The Villanovan cemeteries are especially well known. The main examples are grouped around a hill, now named the Colle della Città, which became the site of the Etruscan city. Like Cerveteri, it lies inland of the coastal plain, some eight kilometres (five miles) from the sea. It is bounded by a steep scarp, which was reinforced by city walls in the fourth century BC. Though the site is now open fields, we know little of the over-all plan of the city in Etruscan times. Much has been overlaid by Roman occupation levels and, apart from the city walls and gates, the only imposing Etruscan monument is the huge temple *podium*, called the Ara Regina. The beautiful terracotta winged horses, now in the Archaeological Museum at Tarquinia, come from this temple (*43*).

Roads led west from the Etruscan city to the neighbouring hill of Monterozzi, where the principal cemetery lay. This hill was once covered by small *tumuli*, covering the simple, rock-cut tombs, made famous by their wall paintings. Intermittent discoveries of these painted chambers have been made over the last two hundred years and more but tombs, previously unrecorded, are still found. Indeed, it might be claimed that, of all Etruscan places, the hill of Monterozzi has been most carefully examined and most enthusiastically described. It is a moving experience to walk from the sunlight down the stepped entrance passage into the cool chamber below and there see upon the walls the fresh paintings, which so vividly depict the Etruscan way of life. In these tombs the people of Tarquinia laid their dead on benches, often in fine sarcophagi, carved with bas-relief and with an effigy of the dead man or woman reclining upon the lid.

Several notable towns are known in the territory of Tarquinia. To the south, two small sites have been excavated recently. The first inhabitants at Luni were of Bronze Age date but houses and defences of the Etruscan period were also found and, at San Giovenale, traces of proto–Villanovan huts were discovered and Etruscan houses, dating from the sixth century BC. Further to the east, in an area probably once disputed with Cerveteri, lies Blera (Bieda), where some two to three thousand small tombs are scattered among the valleys surrounding the medieval town. At the neighbouring site of San Giulano, though a great *tumulus* has recently been unearthed, most of the tombs were cut from the rock sides of the ravine below; their doors and moulded outlines are now thickly overgrown with creepers.

The site of Norchia (?Orcle) has been deserted since Medieval times but here, once again, the Etruscan town was set on the flat surface of rock isolated from the surrounding plateau by the deep ravines cut by streams. The ranks of tombs are particularly impressive and amongst the later examples are some with architectural forms, the columns and pediment carved from the rock; these are now much delapidated but are shown restored by Canina in his drawing (*15*).

The tombs at Castel d'Asso, near Viterbo, are less ambitious; the moulded outlines of false doors indicate the presence of tombs but the vaults were actually entered from narrow passages cut from the rock below. Finally, an interesting group of late tombs has been found at Tuscania, lying barely twenty

15 Canina's illustration of tomb façades at Norchia

kilometres (twelve and a half miles) from Tarquinia up the valley of the Marta.

The Marta River flows from the beautiful Lake of Bolsena, around which lay the territory of ancient Volsinii. Situated to the north of the Faliscan lands and bounded by the Tiber to the east and the territory of Tarquinia and Vulci to the west, was the state of Bolsena (Volsinii), whose principal city should probably be identified with the Etruscan citadel overlooking the modern town on the north east shores of the lake. Pliny noted the wealth of this state and quoted a report that no less than two thousand bronze statues were looted by the Romans, when they sacked the city in 264 BC.† At this time, the site of the city was moved from its commanding position down to the shores of the lake but modern excavation has revealed fine stretches of a city wall set on the hill above, with some of the squared blocks marked with Etruscan letters.

It has also been suggested that ancient Bolsena (Volsinii) should be equated with the Etruscan town at Orvieto, or that this site might once have been called Salpinum, a town mentioned in the ancient sources, when its men joined those of Bolsena (Volsinii) for a raid into Roman territory.† The great

49

cliff-girt rock of Orvieto is, indeed, a magnificent setting for a city (*16*) but, since the medieval and modern town covers the top of the hill, we know little of the Etruscan urban area except for finds of terracottas and the *podium* of a temple, which stands in the small Belvedere Park at the east end of the town.

16 View of Orvieto

Directly below the cliffs on the north side of the hill lies the necropolis of Crocifisso del Tufo, where rows of small tombs, marked by *cippi* and many with the names of their owners written on the lintel above the door, border the neat streets, laid out at right angles to each other. Much debris had fallen from the rock above and covered the tombs, so that a number have been found with their contents intact and these funerary goods are collected in the Archaeological Museum in the town. On the southern flank of the hill was the site of the Cannicella cemetery, where a small sanctuary was also found, in which a nude female statue stood on a round altar, facing a basin for water. Another important group of tombs was discovered in 1863 some five kilometres (three miles) to the south of Orvieto; among this group was the Golini Tomb, sometimes also called Golini Tomb I or the Tomb dei Velii, with a fascinating set of wall paintings, which have been removed to the Archaeological Museum at Florence (*72, 93*).

The territory of Vulci lay between Lake Bolsena and the sea, with the city itself set upon the coastal plain some twenty kilometres (twelve miles) to the north of Tarquinia. In this area, the coastal plain is broad and undulating and the city was situated at a point where the River Fiora met with two of its tributaries, whose steep scarps provided a natural protection for the site. The city had proud memories of its past (p. 27) but otherwise we know nothing of its history until it was defeated by the Romans in 280 BC. The site continued to be occupied through Roman times but now is open fields. In 1956 there began a series of excavations and part of the city is now cleared, including a paved Roman street and the foundations of a temple, which may date back to the sixth century BC. We may hope to learn much of the plan and buildings of a great Etruscan city as these excavations continue. The rich cemeteries, on the other hand, have been robbed down the centuries but excavations only reached a fever pitch after 1828, when a team of oxen fell through the vault of a tomb. Etruscan objects of great worth were found and there followed a ransacking of tombs for goods which might be sold. Huge quantities of antiquities came to light but much irreparable damage was done.

Both Villanovan occupation and graves are known at Vulci and, again, the pattern emerges of several small settlements gradually cohering into a single centre. The tombs show the city was extremely prosperous by the end of the seventh century BC and Vulci was both producing fine work and importing enormous quantities of Greek pottery in the sixth and into the fifth century BC. Ruins of three *tumuli* survive. One, nicknamed the 'Cucumella', is still imposing in its sheer size; originally, a perimeter wall ran round the base of the huge earthen mound, which is over sixty-five metres (seventy yards) in diameter. Most of the tombs, however, are rock-cut, a few with wall paintings. Most famous is the François Tomb, whose chambers were cut from the rock high above the banks of the Fiora; these paintings have been removed to the Torlonia Museum in Rome (p. 27, and *51, 103*).

The territory of Vulci was large and several interesting sites lie within it. An Etruscan cemetery has been found at Poggio Buco and a number of lead sling pellets, marked with the letters *Statnes*; this has led to the suggestion that the site might be identified with that of Statonia, a town in this area to which there are several references in the ancient sources. Poggio Buco appears to have been abandoned in the sixth century and this may also have occurred at Saturnia, where early tombs are known but the walls date from the Hellenistic period. This desertion of smaller sites may well have been the result of the growth in power of the great cities.

The town of Pitigliano is another candidate for identification with ancient Statonia and, near it, lies one of the most delightful of all the minor Etruscan sites; this is Sovana (Suana), now a hamlet which has scarcely changed since the Middle Ages, lying among wooded ravines. Here, carved from the cliffs of tuff, is the most northerly group of Etruscan rock-cut tomb façades and nearby is a roadway, deeply cut into the rock. This is quite a common phenomenon in southern Etruria but often hard to date with any certainty, unless the road is associated with an Etruscan inscription or, as in this case, a tomb door opens on the roadside. Constant use through the centuries has continued to wear away the soft rock, so that a medieval painting, to be seen below the door of the Etruscan tomb, is now well above the modern walking surface (*17*).

On the hill of Ansedonia, lying on the coast just south of the peninsula of Monte Argentario, is the site of the Latin colony of Cosa, settled by the Romans in territory formerly belonging to Vulci. The date of the tremendous walls was long a subject of controversy but Cosa has now been excavated and it is known that they date no earlier than the foundation of the colony in 273 BC. Nevertheless, the colony with its walls, temples and houses gives us an idea what the appearance of a town in Etruria was like during the Hellenistic period and it will be referred to again (p. 73 and *28*).

The northern boundary of Vulci bordered upon that of Roselle (Rusellae), whose great walls encircle a hill-top some ten kilometres (six miles) north-east of Grosseto. Parts of the urban area are now being excavated and an amphitheatre of Imperial date and the Roman Forum, overlying Etruscan buildings, are cleared.

Roselle is now some twenty kilometres (twelve miles) inland but once a large bay, or lagoon, the Lacus Prilius, filled much of the low lying area around Grosseto, serving as a water way for Roselle and for Vetulonia to the north. Though it is now hard to imagine Vetulonia as a maritime power, the typology of the metalwork from the seventh-century graves demonstrates a wide ranging sea trade. A traditional interest in the sea is recalled in the symbolism of a monument set at Cerveteri in

honour of the Emperor Claudius, in which the figure personify-
ing Vetulonia is shown with a steering oar upon his shoulder.
The little modern town stands on the ancient site, crowning
one of a group of hills, which rise steeply from the coastal plain.
A winding road leads up through olive orchards and, as it
reaches the town, one may see an excavated area with a paved
road of Roman date and some houses. A few traces of an
Etruscan wall survive in the town itself and on the surrounding
hills lay some of the richest cemeteries ever dug in Etruria.
There were groups of *pozzetti* and *fosse*, some lying within en-
closing circles of stones; at a later date, chamber tombs were
built, including the Pietrera Tomb, with a square ground plan
rising to a false dome. Many of the objects from these tombs are
now in the Archaeological Museum at Florence. They show an
early prosperity, followed by a decline, beginning as early as
the sixth century BC, and it has been suggested that Vetulonia
fought and was defeated by one of the neighbouring cities, in
all probability Roselle. Later, in Hellenistic times, Vetulonia
regained some of her former prestige.

Unlike most of the coast of Etruria, the promontory of
Piombino offered an admirable site for a city, together with a
sheltered bay. Here, some forty kilometres (twenty-five miles)
to the north of Vetulonia, is the site of Populonia, set upon a
headland overlooking the sea, the only great Etruscan city
placed right upon the coast. Tradition connected it with
Corsica but little is known of the history of Populonia until
it was besieged in the Marian wars of the early first century BC.
It never really recovered from this event and eventually most of
the inhabitants moved down from the citadel to live in the port
area at the foot of the headland. The older cemeteries are
situated around the bay and there have been found both
Villanovan graves and later chamber tombs, some covered with
tumuli. Others were built above the ground and are neat little
rectangular structures, built of fine blocks of cut stone and
roofed with inclining slabs. Some of these tombs were buried in
antiquity beneath a deep layer of industrial debris, accumulated
as a result of iron smelting (p. 145).

There was a general similarity in the fortunes of the great
coastal cities of Etruria. They enjoyed an early prosperity,
based upon the trade brought by the mineral resources found

in their territories. They remained rich and powerful in the sixth century BC, but the decline in Etruscan sea power affected their strength. We do not know when malaria first became endemic in the coastal region of Etruria but it may well be that it, as well as the political effect of the Roman domination and the economic aftermath of the Second Punic War, was responsible for the serious agricultural decline in the second century BC.† By the fifth century AD many of the coastal cities were in ruins and large parts of the region lay in the grip of seasonal malaria, so that it did not regain its former prosperity until the present century.

This history is in strong contrast to that of the inland cities of northern Etruria. Their rise to affluence was less abrupt and, though also industrial, their wealth was principally based on agriculture. Their prosperity has never deserted them and the cities have been continuously occupied and remain thriving centres to this day. The settlement of the northern region was generally less dense than in the south and, in the absence of sites surrounded by cliffs so characteristic of the southern zone, the cities were set upon the summit or steep side of a hill.

The territory of Volterra (Volaterrae) was large and bordered with that of Populonia to the south, Arezzo to the east, while it reached north into the Arno Valley. The graves show that Volterra was occupied in Villanovan times and it is said to have been one of the five cities of the north to make war on Lucius Tarquinius the Elder of Rome.† We know nothing else of its early history and the tombs show no great wealth until the fourth century BC. During the first century BC, survivors of the Marian party were besieged within the walls of the city for two years and Volterra suffered the vengeance of Sulla but it was again a flourishing provincial centre in Imperial times and has been occupied ever since.

It is easy to imagine Volterra withstanding so long a siege. The town stands at the top of a steep-sided hill and may be seen for miles over the rolling landscape. Moreover, the Etruscan city was protected by a formidable circuit of walls, once over six kilometres (four miles) in length. Considerable stretches of these walls still exist, built of enormous squared blocks of stone, whose courses sometimes rise over five metres (five yards) in height (*18*). Two arched gateways survive: most celebrated is

the Porta all'Arco with three heads carved on the stones forming the arch (*19*).

At Volterra, cremation remained the dominant funerary rite
and the ashes of the dead were placed in small chests, or cinerary urns. There was often carved on the lid a miniature effigy
of the dead man or woman, frequently introducing some
personal symbolism (*96*). A wonderful series of these cinerary
chests, carved from the local alabaster, runs through the last
three centuries BC. The reliefs, carved on one or sometimes on

17 Rock-cut roadway near Sovana   *18 City wall of Vol-terra below the church of Santa Chiara*   *19 Porta all'Arco, Volterra*

three sides, may almost stand out in the round and illustrate
scenes taken from Greek mythology or aspects of local life,
showing the gradual assimilation into the Roman world which
was taking place at this time. Unrobbed tombs have been
found with family groups of these urns, placed on the bench
around the wall. One, the Inghirami Tomb, has been reconstructed in the garden of the Archaeological Museum at
Florence and another, belonging to the great Caecina family,
some of whose members Cicero counted among his friends, was
opened in 1739. The cinerary chests formed the nucleus of the
present charming Archaeological Museum in the town.

The other great cities of northern Etruria lay in the basin of
the upper Tiber and its tributaries. This is one of the most
beautiful and fertile of all the regions of Italy, with rich pas-
tures and fields of corn and the hillsides covered with olive
orchards and vineyards. The valley of the Chiana forms a link

between the basin of the upper Tiber and the valley of the Arno, and here lay Chiusi (Clusium), whose territory was bounded by that of Roselle and Bolsena to the west and south and by Cortona and Perugia to the north and east. The city became prominent in Roman history with the story of Lars Porsenna and it is perfectly possible that, towards the end of the sixth century BC, Chiusi had begun to rival the southern and coastal cities in wealth and power. There had been the recent expansion into the Po Valley and the agriculture must already have been well developed, as corn supplies were being shipped to Rome on the Tiber early in the fifth century BC, while at Chiusi the tombs show a growing prosperity and artistic activity.†

Little is known of the Etruscan city at Chiusi, which lies buried beneath the modern town. The Poggio Gaiella, some five kilometres (three miles) from Chiusi, is a hill-top site about fifteen metres (fifty feet) in height and two hundred and seventy-five metres (three hundred yards) in circumference encircled by a perimeter wall. The interior is hollowed into a series of tombs, in some cases linked by winding passages.

There are, too, painted tombs scattered among the hillsides around Chiusi. At Colle Casuccini, the entrance passage leads horizontally into the side of the hill and at the end of the passage stand two stone slabs, set upon pivots. These are the original doors of the tomb, which still swing open to allow the visitor to stoop and enter the rock-cut chamber and admire the scenes painted on the walls around him (20). Another notable tomb is that of the Grand Duke, which has a perfect barrel vault; here, the cinerary chests have been left in position, dating the tomb to the second century BC (21).

Chiusi had been occupied by the Villanovans and like the Volterrans, the people continued to cremate the dead; over the centuries they used a fascinating variety of forms for the urns and cinerary chests and a large collection may be seen in the Archaeological Museum in the town (29, 30, 40). Both the shape of these chests and the charming bas-reliefs carved upon them and on other types of memorial, offer much information about contemporary life and customs and they will be frequently mentioned in the following pages (37, 98, 99, 111).

The three great Etruscan cities lying to the north and east of Chiusi, that is, Perugia (Perusia), Cortona and Arezzo

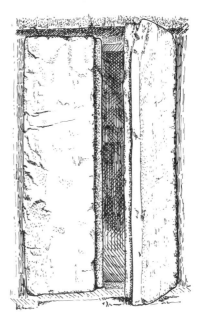

20 Door of the Colle Casuccini
    Tomb, Chiusi

21 Interior of the Tomb of the Grand Duke, Chiusi

(Arretium) shared a similar setting and history. Their territories lay between the curve of the Umbrian Apennines to the east and the fertile valleys and plain encircling Lake Trasimeno to the west. Cortona was particularly rich in foundation stories, some suggesting a mythical antiquity; Perugia, especially, must have had to contend with the Umbrians for the possession of her territory.

It is hard to be precise about the development of this region, which, in the sixth century, was probably still overshadowed by the early power of Chiusi, yet, by tradition, Perugia was involved in the colonial expansion into the Po Valley. There is more evidence for an extensive Etruscan occupation by the fifth century and certainly these cities, together with Chiusi, must have withstood the first impact of the Gauls. They fought the Romans, when they broke into the upper Tiber Valley in 310 BC, and Livy describes them at this time as among the foremost states of Etruria.† By 280 BC, they with the other Etruscan cities, had submitted to the Romans but they did not revolt even when Hannibal with his Carthaginian army marched past their walls and routed the Roman legions by the shores of Lake Trasimeno. Perugia suffered especially in the Civil Wars of the first century BC but all three cities were flourishing regional centres in the Imperial period, as they still are today, so that we have little knowledge of the Etruscan remains, which must lie buried under the modern towns.

At Perugia (Perusia), parts of the Etruscan city wall survive and two gateways, the so-called Arch of Augustus and the Porta Marzia, have been much restored. A large number of tombs have been found in the vicinity and many of the urns and other tomb goods have been gathered into the Archaeological Museum of the town. Most outstanding of these tombs is that of the Volumnii family. This tomb has some very fine architectural detail and several exceptionally splendid cinerary chests; they date to the second half of the second and the first century BC and the final inscriptions, bilingual with Latin, demonstrate the disuse of the Etruscan language at this time.

Stretches of great city walls may be seen at Cortona, encircling the steep-sided hill on which the city stands. At the foot of the hill lies the Melon of Camuscia, a large *tumulus* covering chambers built of dry stone walling and dated to the seventh century BC, while on the hillside nearer the city is the so-called 'Cave of Pythagoras', a chamber tomb with a circular ground plan, which was probably built in the fourth century BC (*22*). Even the location of Etruscan Arezzo (Arretium) has been doubted but fifth-century and later temple terracottas have been found there, as well as late tombs. A wall of brick, discovered under the modern town, may be an unusual fortification.†

22 The 'Cave of Pythagoras', Cortona

The valley of the Arno with the foothills of the Apennines to the north always formed the frontier between the Etruscans and the fierce Ligurian tribes, but neither the Villanovan nor the early Etruscan occupation of this area is yet clearly understood, nor the status of Pisa, on the north side of the mouth of the Arno. There is evidence for Etruscan penetration, especially into the valleys of the southern tributaries of the middle Arno and into the Arno Valley itself (as is shown by the fine tomb, with an Etruscan inscription, at Quinto Fiorentino, dated as early as the seventh century BC). This was followed by a scattered settlement, perhaps representing isolated farming communities. Undoubtedly, much of the area lay within the influence of Volterra, which affected the style of the early *stelai* at Fiesole (Faesulae). Yet this town, set upon the summit of the hill immediately to the north of Florence, does not appear to have been settled until the third century BC. It is first mentioned in the campaign which led up to the battle with the Gauls at Talamone in 225 BC and, no doubt, the fine circuit of town walls was a defence against the Gaulish tribes, as well as the Ligurian peoples. In the first century BC, the town suffered in the Social War and later became a headquarters of Catiline's conspiracy; the site is now within the suburban area of Florence but, where the ancient settlement has not been overlaid by medieval or modern buildings, both Etruscan remains and ruins of Imperial date have been uncovered, including a temple of the Hellenistic period, built in the third and restored in the first century BC.†

Though, traditionally, there were twelve Etruscan cities founded in the Po Valley, few sites have yielded substantial evidence from this period. Traces of the Villanovan occupation have been discovered under the modern city of Bologna but almost nothing is known of the Etruscan colony (Felsina). However, the rich cemeteries show that the Etruscans were established there by about 525 BC and a delightful series of funeral *stelai* runs through the fifth and into the fourth century (*84*). Goods reached Bologna from Etruria and, in quantity, from Greece and the latter must have been imported at Spina, the Adriatic port lying to the south of the mouth of the Po. This town, whose origins were attributed in antiquity to a wide variety of peoples, appears to have been settled towards the end of the sixth century. Certainly it was an exceptionally mixed community, whose members, like those of the port of Adria to the north, were drawn together by their common interest in trade; during the fifth and fourth centuries BC, both Greeks and Etruscans lived at Spina, which had a treasury at Delphi.†

The site was silted over in the gradual growth of the Po delta and was already far inland in Strabo's time. It was only rediscovered during modern drainage of the marshes; excavation of the cemeteries began in 1922 and the graves, lying intact in the deep mud, have now yielded what is probably the largest number of Attic vases from any single site and Etruscan objects as well. With the aid of air photography, the plan of Spina has been established; like ancient Ravenna and modern Venice, it was built upon wooden piles and the canals, serving as streets, were laid out upon a rectilinear pattern, while a broad channel connected the port to the sea.

A strict grid plan for the streets was used at Marzabotto, an Etruscan colonial site, lying some twenty-five kilometres (fifteen miles) to the south of Bologna in the valley of the Reno, one of the main routes south over the Apennines. The history of the town was short; settled on a virgin site in about 500 BC, it was sacked by the Gauls in the fourth century and was never re-occupied, so the town lies open to excavation. This was begun during the last century and much of the site now lies exposed; here, then, is an admirable place to begin a description of the town planning and architecture of the Etruscans.

5

Town planning and architecture; sculpture and painting

As the creative genius of the Greeks grew to its full power, the peoples of the Mediterranean fell more and more under the domination of Greek art. Among them were the Etruscans, who throughout the period of their independent artistic expression were profoundly influenced by their Greek neighbours and contemporaries. Nevertheless, the architecture, sculpture and painting in Etruria reflect the differing personality and circumstances of the Etruscans which inevitably imposed a quite individual treatment of these art forms. Although they may follow Greek styles, themes and even details, the Etruscans used them for their own requirements and within a regional interpretation, often that of a single city-state.

TOWN PLANNING

From Greek and Roman authors, we know that the Etruscans used certain rites at the founding of their cities and that they were used at the foundation of Rome.† Before we examine the archaeological record, which is the main source of information on town planning, it will be useful to describe these rites.

First an ideal point was chosen, a pit dug and offerings thrown in; from this point, the perimeter of the city walls was marked out. Then the founder, taking a plough with a bronze share, yoked a bull and a cow and ploughed a furrow along the line where the walls were to be built, lifting the plough across the places reserved for gateways. The clods were carefully laid on the inner side of the furrow, thus creating a symbolic moat and wall; subsequently the *pomoerium*, an open space both within and outside the walls, remained sacred and no one could build or plough within it. The Romans believed that their own formula for laying out of colonies and camps went back to Etruscan tradition. First, auspices, or omens, were taken by an augur, then the site was oriented to the points of the compass and the main streets laid out, using a surveying instrument called a *groma*. The word *groma*, and probably the instrument itself, was derived from the Greeks, but reached the Romans from an Etruscan intermediary. Roman sources also mention that the Etruscans believed no city to be complete without three gates, three streets and three temples, dedicated to Jupiter, Juno and Minerva and that the temples of Venus, Vulcan and Mars should lie outside the walls.†

The development from Villanovan villages to planned city building was, naturally, very gradual. In the course of time, some villages in especially favourable positions amalgamated into towns and, as the last chapter has shown, these towns were provided with defences, as circumstances dictated. Such towns would tend to dominate their districts and it seems that at least by the end of the seventh century BC the idea of the city-state had emerged. Like Rome, many of the older Etruscan centres were set on sites totally unsuitable for ideal organization and, moreover, their growth was spread over several centuries, so it is not surprising to find little evidence of large-scale grid planning among them. At Rome, some important steps towards the creation of the central urban nucleus were traditionally credited to the regal period, when Etruscan influence was very strong. These achievements included the building of the Capitoline Temple, the construction of encircling fortifications and the draining of the Forum. At first, this was probably with ditches, some perhaps covered, which were later enlarged into the *Cloaca Maxima*, whose arched exit upon the Tiber may still be seen today.

By the sixth century BC, however, the Etruscans did use grid planning, where opportunity arose. There is evidence for this from the old centres of Etruria, like the necropolis at Orvieto, where the tombs are laid out along neat streets, which cross each other at right-angles, or at Cerveteri (Caere), where some tombs are grouped in straight streets or, occasionally, in squares. But the greatest possibilities were offered by the new colonial sites and, in Campania, the grid plan of the streets at ancient

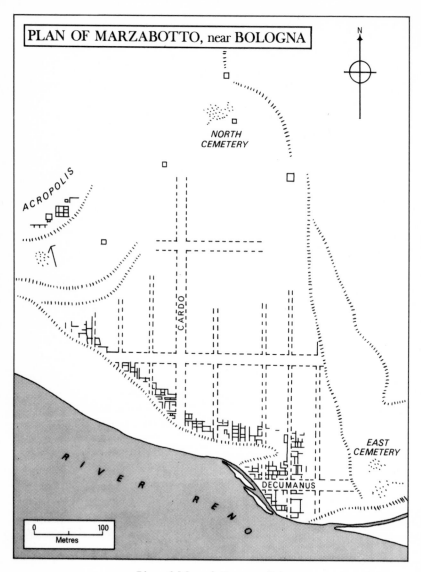

23 *Plan of Marzabotto, near Bologna*

Capua (modern Santa Maria di Capua Vetere) is believed to be of Etruscan origin. In the north, the rectilinear pattern of the canals at Spina has already been mentioned, but by far the most complete evidence for Etruscan town planning comes from the excavations at Marzabotto (p. 61, *23*).

This colony was placed upon a flat gravel site beside the River Reno, which has now eroded much of the southern end of the ancient town. The streets are arranged in a rigid grid plan, carefully oriented to the points of the compass. Unlike the usual Roman division into quarters by two major streets, the *cardo* and *decumanus*, running north to south and east to west respectively, the *cardo* at Marzabotto is intersected at right angles by three *decumani*, which are in turn linked by smaller streets, running parallel with the *cardo*; this systematic plan was modelled on that of Greek colonial cities of Magna Graecia (6). Both *cardo* and *decumani* are very broad, some fifteen metres (sixteen yards) in width, while the small streets are five metres (five and a half yards) wide. The main streets had pavements on either side, cobbled with river stones, and there were occasional sets of stepping-stones across the roads.

The houses were grouped in an individual and irregular manner within the rectangular blocks outlined by the streets. Only the footings of the walls survive, built of river stones, for the walls themselves were of unfired brick. The houses were probably of a single storey only; both flat and curved tiles were found in the excavations. The house plans differ greatly; in one example, a wide passage led from the street into an interior courtyard, which was surrounded by a series of rooms. Both the supply and drainage of water were well managed at Marzabotto; a small cistern, fed through stone blocks cut as pipes, was found on the neighbouring hillside and terracotta pipes, circular in section and designed to join with other lengths, were discovered *in situ* among the houses.

Many of the houses had deep wells, lined with dry stone walling, within the courtyards; the mouths of some wells were covered with stone slabs, pierced with a round hole, but a fine terracotta well-head was also found. Drains led from the houses and ran along the sides of the streets in deep ditches, with sides lined by dry stone walling, and covered with large slabs of stone. The habitation area, shops and working space seem to have been mingled at Marzabotto. Spindle-whorls and loom-weights testify to local weaving and a potters' quarter was recognized from kilns and a number of small pottery discs, used for keeping the vases apart as they were fired. Stones, marked as weights, were found and both tools and slag, found in some of the houses, show that they were used as metal workshops. The religious centre of the town lay on a small summit just to the north west of the inhabited area; this hill was crowned with five sacred structures, aligned with the street plan and facing south. One was a raised platform with moulded sides and there were temples, both with a single *cella* and of tripartite form. Two cemeteries lay to the north and east of the town; the tombs were built of stone slabs, forming boxes and were surmounted by *cippi*.

ARCHITECTURE

Many references have already been made to the city walls and tombs of the Etruscan cities. Of all their monuments, these have most often survived and are the most constant witnesses of the activities of the Etruscans.

The architecture of the tombs shows that masonry was used by the seventh century BC to build false vaults and false arches and that the true barrel vault was developed by Hellenistic times. The oldest defensive fortifications of which we know in Etruria is the earthwork at Poggio Buco, dated to the seventh century BC. The earliest city wall in stone is that of Roselle, built in the sixth century BC. These great walls have a very rough appearance, constructed of huge, irregular blocks, often with wide fissures between the joints. At Veii, the city wall of fine, squared masonry was backed by a rampart of earth; this wall was not built until the fifth century and other walls with similar masonry, set in courses and without mortar, are not considered prior to this date. Polygonal masonry, in which the face of large irregular blocks was flattenened and their edges fitted close together, may be seen at Cosa and various other sites (*28*). This technique was once thought to denote a high antiquity but it is now believed to have been introduced into Etruria during the Hellenistic period. To this period, too, belong the addition of wall turrets and arched gateways, which, with battlements and wooden gates, are sometimes seen on contemporary representations, like a relief from Volterra, dating to the third or second century BC, which illustrates the legendary siege of Thebes, but borrows local details (*24*).

Unlike the construction of their city walls and tombs, the Etruscans did not habitually use stone for their temples, except in building the foundations or *podium*. This characteristic may

24 Relief showing a siege scene in Volterra Archaeological Museum

well have sprung from a religious feeling for the material, influenced by very archaic types of temple, Italic or Greek, which were built of wood and from the availability of fine timber. Throughout their history, the Etruscans continued to to use wood for the superstructure of their temples and, consequently, these have not survived, as the beautiful stone architecture of the Greek world has done. The Etruscans did, however, cover the wooden elements of the temples with terracotta, using this medium both as a protection and for decoration, and the long series of temple terracottas, which often survive and have frequently been mentioned above, provide much evidence both for the development of sculpture and, with the stone foundations, for the appearance of the temples.

From early times in Italy, the gods were worshipped and auspices taken in open air sanctuaries. A model of a raised platform, approached by a flight of steps and surrounded with a moulded edge, is known from Chiusi and probably represents an architectural form of such a precinct (25). Similar structures are extant, including the example on the hill-top at Marzabotto and it is difficult not to believe that these were open precincts for worship and the taking of auspices. The building of temples, the dwelling in which the image of the god was placed, came with a more anthropomorphic religious conception, when the gods were represented in human form; as yet, we know of no temples dating to the seventh century but an example with a single *cella*, the enclosed room for the image of the god, has been found on the acropolis at Veii, which dates to the first half or middle of the sixth century BC. This building was just over eight by fifteen metres (eight and a half by sixteen yards), but soon very different proportions were being used.

The sanctuary of Portonaccio at Veii is known to have been used in the seventh century from the date of the votive offerings dedicated by the worshippers, which have been found there, but the temple itself was not built until the end of the sixth century BC. The stone foundations have a square ground plan, each side measuring eighteen and a half metres (twenty yards), and thus totally unlike the ground plan of Greek temples; the position of the temple walls is not certain but is likely that it was divided into three *cellae*, the tripartite form characteristic of Tuscan temples.

Vitruvius gives details of the style and proportions of these temples. The foundations for the temple should be almost square, though slightly longer than it is wide, and the front half should be a porch with columns. At the back there should be three rooms; the central *cella* should be slightly larger than the two spaces on either side, which could either be *cellae*, entered by doors, or open wings. The porch should have two lines of four columns, placed in line with the walls at the back. Vitrivius also noted that the frontal elevation of Tuscan temples, with their wooden beams covered in terracotta decoration, had a broad, top-heavy appearance.† The foundation walls of Temple A at Pyrgi show this type of arrangement, though in this case there were three rows of columns in the porch (26).

25 *Model in Chiusi Archaeological Museum*

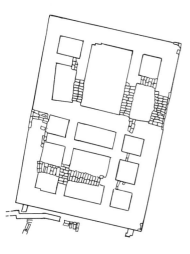

26 *Plan of the foundations of Temple A at Pyrgi*

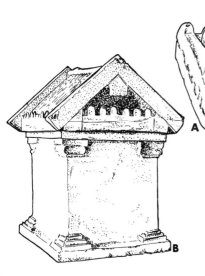

27A *Lid of a stone cinerary chest, showing the arrangement of tiles and antefixes.* B *Terracotta cinerary chest, showing the arrangement of beams*

From this and other temples, it is clear that Vitruvius' description is an accurate systemization of the prostyle temples of Etruria, though these were naturally built with many variations.

The temples were approached from the front only, a point well shown at the Belvedere temple of Orvieto, which has a fine flight of steps leading up from a frontal precinct, enclosed by a wall. Unlike the customary construction of unfired brick, the walls of the temple at Fiesole were built of stone (p. 60); we also know from this temple that an arrangement with the columns standing between a continuation of the side walls of the wings, projected forward onto the porch, was sometimes used in Etruria, as were temples with a single *cella*.

The characteristic columns of these temples, often of wood, were without fluting and had a collar and cushion capital. The Etruscans were also fond of using Aeolic capitals with leaflike volutes, and Ionic forms are also represented (*28, 29, 73*). Following Greek models, the Etruscans used roofing tiles for their temples, the large flat *tegulae* overlapped by the curved *imbrices*, covering the joints. At the eaves, marking the end of the lines of *imbrices*, were placed the antefixes (*27A*). These terracottas were often moulded in the form of a human head and, when the temple grew in size, the heads were surrounded by a shell motive and replaced by whole figures and other decorations. The exposed wooden elements of the temples were also covered with terracotta, principally the architrave, or beam running across the top of the columns, the rafters of the gables and the ends of the ceiling beams (*27B*). Along the horizontal elements ran a frieze, at first often a repeating pattern of groups of gods or men, seated or in procession, but later frequently an elegant floral motif. Terracotta figures were sometimes placed on the roof of temples. Unlike the Greeks, the Etruscans often left the pediment, or triangular space beneath the gable, open in front, and they did not fill this space with figures until the Hellenistic period (*27B, 28*). All these terracotta decorations were painted, often in many colours, so that the temples must indeed have had a brilliant effect. The type of temple with terracotta sculpture was used by the Romans as well as the Etruscans and continued to be built down to the first century BC. A reconstruction of the temples on the acropolis of Cosa shows the style used about 100 BC (*28*).†

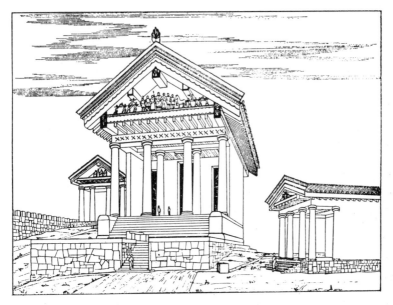

28 Reconstruction of temples on the acropolis of Cosa, circa *100* BC

29A Cinerary chest from Chiusi in the form of a house. B Cinerary chest in the form of a house in Florence Archaeological Museum

Until more excavation has been done in the towns and cities of Etruria, we shall continue to know little of the other public buildings until the Hellenistic period; most of the information now available comes from Cosa, where a colonnade, council chamber and assembly hall were grouped around the central square or Forum. Theatres and amphitheatres known in Etruria all lie outside our period and the scenes on contemporary reliefs or the terracotta models, like those of a free-standing tower and a colonnade recently found at Vulci, only underline our ignorance.

More excavation is also needed before we fully understand the development of the house in Etruria, though in this case much useful information comes from the rock-cut tombs, especially those of Cerveteri. Villanovan huts have been described and the internal features of a hut, with a central beam and a roof sloping down to low walls, are reproduced in the rock-cut Tomb of the Hut, dated to the seventh century BC, which lies within the great Tumulus II in the Banditaccia cemetery at Cerveteri (*13,2*). By the sixth century BC, houses were being built on rectilinear lines, sometimes with cut stone foundations; the courtyard houses of Marzabotto will be remembered and it is likely that many people continued to live in such houses until the end of the Etruscan period.

However, more complex forms were also developed, some of which inevitably recall the plan of the Tuscan temple. Recent excavations at Acqua Rossa near Viterbo have brought to light a part of the town which was destroyed about 500 BC; foundations of houses were found with three parallel rooms at the back, opening onto a vestibule. This ground plan is also known from the tombs; an example, the Tomb of the Grecian Vases, lies under Tumulus II of the Banditaccia cemetery (*13,3*), and has an entrance passage, with a room on either side, which leads into a wide central vestibule or hall; at the back are three parallel rooms, each furnished with funerary couches. Other tombs show variants upon this plan; sometimes, the central door at the back is larger or this entrance reaches to the full height of the roof and is as wide as the room beyond, while a false door at the back shows a further exit is imagined.

This plan, with three rooms at the back, was followed in the Volumnii Tomb, which is generally dated to the second century BC; it is clear that it represents a type of house also known at Pompeii and the well-to-do Roman's home, as described by Vitruvius. In a Roman house, the central hall was called the *cavaedium* or *atrium*. The *atrium* could either be fully roofed, or displuviate, that is, with an opening to the sky and with the slope of the roof shedding the rain-water outwards, or the *atrium* could be impluviate, with an opening to the sky and with the roof shedding the rain-water inwards into a central pool.† Unlike the other impluviate types, the roof of the *atrium tuscanicum* was upheld by beams set into the walls, a form which the Etruscans, with their fondness of heavy woodwork, might well employ. The tombs furnish no early evidence for impluviate *atria*; however, the Mercareccia Tomb at Tarquinia and a cinerary chest from Chiusi do show an opening in the roof (*29A*).

The earliest known example of a house with an *atrium tuscanicum* is at Cosa and dated to the second century BC. Emeline Richardson has pointed out that this is essentially an urban form, implying a difficulty in placing windows in the outer walls of a house and has also noted its utility as a water supply. No wells were found on the hill top of Cosa and the rain-water was collected from the roof of buildings and stored in vaulted cisterns. There seems, then, little doubt that the Roman house with a central hall, three rooms at the back and a garden beyond, was anticipated in Etruscan forms and that the impluviate *atrium*, though not necessarily invented in Etruria, was a development of the Hellenistic period, shared by the Etruscans, who created a special form. This would agree with the description given by Diodorus, that the Etruscans used the central space of their houses to shield the masters, who would use the inner rooms, from the noise of their many servants, who would have the rooms at the entrance.†

The tombs also provide many details of the internal construction of the houses and of their furnishings, which will be considered below. The doorways are sometimes arched but are usually shown with a heavy lintel across the top overlapping the two jambs at either side, which slope outwards towards the bottom (*47*). The windows are sometimes arched, though many are rectilinear in shape. In the Tomb of the Capitals at Cerveteri (*13,4*), the architectural features of the roof are cut from the rock; two columns support the beams of the vestibule, joists are shown laid across the beams and, above these, there appears to be thatching. Shingles may also have been used and tiles appear by the sixth century BC. The evidence for the external appearance of the houses is less full, though the rock-cut façades of some tombs must bear them a resemblance and we have a number of cinerary chests, mainly from Chiusi, carved as houses or with representations of houses in bas-relief. These occasionally show house fronts with two columns; an example has an open loggia, set high upon the roof, and one cinerary chest, now in the Archaeological Museum in Florence, is carved to show a monumental doorway, pilasters and fine stone work, details which have been likened to the architecture of the Renaissance palaces of that city (*29B*).

SCULPTURE

Greatly differing judgments have been passed upon the Etruscan achievement in sculpture and painting. Historians of art may sincerely admire some masterpieces, or acknowledge the fine craftsmanship and the Etruscans' good taste in emulating the Greeks, but they seldom give unreserved praise. Paradoxically, it is the very merit of Etruscan art which has been the chief cause of this censure; had their works only been comparable with those of their Italic neighbours, the critics would have expected little and been less severe. It is a mark of the standard of Etruscan art that it must be studied with that of Greece, even if such a comparison is to its disadvantage. That the Etruscans were not rivals of the Greeks at the height of their creative power can scarcely be held to their discredit and that they consistently followed Greek styles may be viewed with disdain or approval. To these incoming influences they brought their own traditions, skills, character and needs and it is the fusion between the foreign and the native currents which forms the mainspring of Etruscan art.

Such borrowing, however, held inherent dangers. Etruscan art, following Greek styles and themes but without the intellectual and historic stimuli which inspired them, often appears lacking in comprehension and unity; unlike Greek art, there is no consistent mean and excellence and poor quality are often found close together. The Greeks sought to express the sublime and the eternal through harmony and idealization, especially of the human body, whereas the Etruscans seemed disinterested in generalization and in abstract ideas and so used the Greek forms to convey their own inclination towards the particular and the personal, often emphasizing the temporary and expressive detail. It is for this reinterpretation and self-expression that we must chiefly look in studying Etruscan art and, to begin this survey, we must now return to the eighth and seventh centuries BC, when Greek styles had not yet begun to dominate the local art forms.

The early Villanovans had made only minor attempts to express themselves in representational art and were more at home with the repetitive, geometric patterns which are familiar from their pottery and engraved bronzes, and with an iconography inherited from central Europe. As the eighth century BC progressed, an increasing number of foreign goods reached them by sea from the east and the Villanovans responded by enlarging their repertoire, both with new objects, new motifs and new manners of dealing with them; contemporary Villanovan bronzes often copy types from the east Mediterranean but were frequently influenced by the Geometric style of Greece as well, and sometimes local traditional forms were also grafted on. Such mingling may be seen in the design of the Bisenzio wheeled-stand (7), a local work of the early seventh century BC, made by a smith already capable of casting groups of animals and human figures with some competence.

The full Orientalizing period of the seventh century brought a wide selection of imports to Etruria. Amongst them were objects of precious metals, engraved with scenes from real life or fiction, and a large number of bronzes either cast, repoussé or engraved, from objects serving many functions. Many wooden objects were probably imported and also woven fabrics, about which we know so little. There is, too, a strong probability that refugee craftsmen arrived from the east and carved ivories in Etruria, for these show a strong stylistic influence from the east Mediterranean. The impact of this deluge of new motifs and forms was overwhelming to a culture with no tenacious local tradition in the representational arts. The Etruscan craftsmen borrowed from all these sources, copying, adapting, mingling

75

motifs and transposing materials and finally they produced so rich a mixture that it became a style in its own right. This artistic activity was almost entirely confined to small objects, personal possessions and funerary goods, but though the modelling was worked in a small scale, it was nevertheless the first sculptural style of the Etruscans.

One form of sculpture in Etruria during the seventh century BC appears to have had an entirely local inspiration; at Chiusi,

30 Cinerary urn, with a lid modelled as a human head, in Chiusi Archaeological Museum

31 Terracotta seated figure from Cerveteri in the British Museum

cinerary urns of pottery or bronze had lids modelled as human heads; at first the style was very tentative but some fine examples were produced in the late seventh and sixth centuries (*30*). These 'Canopic urns', as they are termed, were often placed on model chairs of a local type and a table was sometimes set before them.

Towards the end of the seventh century BC the artists of Etruria were turning to projects on a larger scale, though sometimes still inspired by small imported objects. Tradition recalls that Demaratus brought modellers with him from Corinth in the middle of the seventh century.† Whatever the truth behind this story, sculpture on a larger scale began about this time; three terracotta figures, some fifty centimetres (twenty inches) in height, have been found in a tomb at Cerveteri, which, to judge by the jewellery they wear, must date as early as the second half of the seventh century (*31*). Stone sculpture in Etruria dates from the Pietrera Tomb at Vetulonia. These life-size figures are much damaged and only the heads are carved fully in the round but they show Orientalizing motifs, allied with Greek details.

Between 625 and 575 BC, taste in Etruria swung decisively towards Greek models, themselves now free from any dependence upon the art of the east Mediterranean world, and, at a date roundly placed at 600 BC, Etruria entered the Archaic period, which was to last down to about 475 BC. It is possible to define more closely the various artistic influences which were arriving from the Greek world at this time.

Throughout the seventh and to about the middle of the sixth century BC, Corinthian pottery dominated the market. From the middle of the sixth century, Etruria received strong artistic impulses from the Greek cities of Asia Minor; Ionian taste was also widely accepted in the Greek world during this period and a considerable trade passed to Sybaris and the west. Moreover, the Phocaeans were then colonizing in the west Mediterranean and Ionian craftsmen, refugees from the troubled conditions in their homeland, settled and worked in Etruria (p. 106). These currents combined to create those 'eastern elements', noted in Etruscan culture of the sixth century BC, which have been considered to be evidence for a migration from the east. As the sixth century progressed, the importation of Attic black-figure pottery began to supersede that of Corinth and, by 500 BC, red-figure pottery from Athens began to reach Etruria; from this time, the art of Athens became the dominant Greek influence among the Etruscans, as it also was in the Greek world.

The Etruscans, though consistently following these styles, maintained their own characteristics; as with their architecture, both religious traditions and practical considerations played a part in the choice of materials they used for their sculpture. In Etruria, sculpture in stone was reserved for funerary monuments. Moreover, like Magna Graecia, local sources of marble were rare and, since the quarries of Carrara were not exploited until the first century BC, the Etruscan sculptors worked in the less beautiful medium of the regional types of stone. Thus when one thinks of Etruscan sculpture it is largely of the bronzes and terracottas, which emerge as traditional means of expression in Etruria. This forms a deep contrast with the sculpture of Greece.†

The Archaic period was one of great prosperity for the Etruscans. The cities were rich and powerful, direct contact with Campania brought new artistic currents, largely shared by the people of southern Lazio, and, throughout the sixth century BC, the spirit expressed in Greek painted pottery and other art forms seems to have been easily assimilated by the Etruscans into their own confident mood of the time. The moment was favourable for artists and they, in their turn, were fully capable of depicting the prevailing spirit in an exuberant style, which has often been considered to be the most attractive ever produced in Etruria.

The cities of Etruria were producing extremely individual art forms and styles during the Archaic period. At Tarquinia, a number of stone bas-reliefs have been found, some of which recall Corinthian designs; the scenes are divided into panels and fabulous monsters are depicted or events from real life, some introducing a narrative element (*32*). A splendid leopard, which might once have formed part of a lintel over the door of a tomb, comes from Vulci (*33*). A number of statues, carved in the round from local stone, are known from this site and they were originally placed outside the doors of tombs, as guardian figures. This series includes a charming statue of a boy, riding

32 Stone bas-relief in Tarquinia Archaeological Museum

on a dolphin or some sea-monster, winged lions, sphinxes, and a fine centaur, whose stiff pose and features show the influence of the early Archaic style of Greek sculpture. Many of these statues may be dated to the first half of the sixth century BC but the series of tomb guardians continued after this time. Stone statues, in related styles, were also set up outside tombs at Veii, Orvieto and Chiusi.

Another statue from Vulci may be mentioned; it was found in the Isis Tomb, whose contents are now in the British Museum. It is the figure of a woman, carved in gypsum and somewhat over eighty centimetres (thirty-two inches) in height; the style, particularly of the head with enormous eyes and low brow, together with the rigid, frontal pose, emphasized by the strong,

33 Leopard, carved in stone, from Vulci. In the Museum of Fine Arts, Boston, William Francis Warden Fund

79

vertical lines of the draped body, also demonstrates the influence of Archaic sculpture of Greece. This figure has been dated near the middle of the sixth century BC, but, during the later part of the Archaic period, the sculptors of Etruria were growing increasingly concerned with introducing movement into their designs.

A number of fine bronze objects have also been found at Vulci, which was probably the centre of a school of bronzework producing many types of household furniture during the later sixth and fifth centuries BC. These bronzes often have small human figures, cast in the round, worked into the design (*61A, 62*); some of these figures are now shown in vigorous action and show so completely a mastery of the craft that they were much admired and widely exported. Chuisi had a contemporary school of bronzework and, in Campania, particularly fine bronze urns were produced and decorated with lively figures, closely allied in style to that of the Greeks.

The Etruscans also used another bronzeworking technique with great skill; sheet bronze was hammered from the back to create repoussé decorations and these were used as part of pieces of household furniture and to cover wooden objects as

34 Chariot with bronze decorations from Monteleone. In the Metropolitan Museum of Art, New York, Rogers Fund (1903)

35 Terracotta sarcophagus from Cerveteri in the Villa Giulia Museum, Rome

large as carts or chariots, like the magnificent example found
at Monteleone in Umbria (*34*). This masterpiece, and a related
group of repoussé bronzes, have a style with flowing lines and
active figures with rounded forms, a style strongly influenced
by Ionian art. Their place of manufacture is debated but it
may well be that these bronzes were made in southern Etruria
during the third quarter of the sixth century, when the Archaic
style was becoming mature. Ionian influence may also be seen
in the modelling of the fine terracotta sarcophagus from
Cerveteri, now in the Villa Giulia Museum; it is lifesize and
shows a contented married couple, gently smiling and reclining
upon a high couch and it is usually dated to about 520 BC (*35*).
   The second great school of Archaic terracotta sculpture was
at Veii, where terracotta had been used for the decoration of
temples since at least the middle of the sixth century BC. This
form of art was particularly associated with the name of Vulca
and the beautiful statues found at the Portonaccio sanctuary
have been attributed to his school (p. 45). This group of four
nearly life-size statues, dated about 500 BC, probably all stood
on the ridge-beam of the temple's roof and represented the

story of Apollo's struggle with Hercules over the hind, or deer, which was sacred to Artemis. The statues are incomplete but the stocky figure of Hercules survives, the bound hind at his feet, with a menacing Apollo, striding towards him, the smiling head of Mercury (Greek Hermes) and a goddess with a child in her arms.

The group is a masterpiece; Apollo's rapid movement is emphasized by his pose and draperies, clinging about him, while an intense quality is conveyed by the modelling of both the figures and faces, as if all were frozen at a moment of strong emotion. The bronze Capitoline Wolf, among the most celebrated statues from antiquity, also has this tense stance (*36*); her lean, muscular body has been likened to the bound hind of the Veii group and it may well be that this emblem of Rome was created by the school of Veii, sometime early in the fifth century BC.

Fine terracottas of late Archaic date are also known from

36 The Capitoline Wolf in the Palazzo dei Conservatori, *Capitoline Museum, Rome*

37 Cinerary chest with a bas-relief of a banqueting scene in Chiusi Archaeological Museum

Civita Castellana (*82*) and other sites in southern Etruria and Lazio. The majority of Etruscan sculpture known from this period comes from the south but the northern region was developing and, in particular, the city of Chiusi was growing in wealth and power. Here, towards the end of the sixth century BC, there begins a charming series of bas-reliefs, carved in the fine grained local limestone, mainly on cinerary chests and *cippi*; the style is pleasantly rustic and all sorts of animated scenes are shown, in which we see weddings and processions, war and funerals, as well as gay banquets and sports (*37, 98, 99, 111*). These reliefs, like the *stelai* of Bologna, continued through the fifth century BC, but their style changed very gradually, for long retaining an Archaic flavour.

Several inter-related causes may be put forward to explain the general tendency in Etruria to repeat the formulae of Archaic art at a time when Greek styles had passed first to the Severe and then the full Classical style of Periclean Athens. There can be little doubt that trade declined in the Tyrrhenian Sea after 474 BC, the year in which the Etruscans were decisively defeated at sea off Cuma by the Syracusan fleet. Campania was lost to the Etruscans and the fifth century brought them other military reverses, which may, in turn, have caused an economic recession; moreover, Greek art had moved into fields where the Etruscans were not fully prepared to follow. We have less evidence for work in the early Classical style than of Archaic art, yet there were some notable achievements; examples of fine terracotta sculpture continue, and outstanding among them is the beautiful and intricate group which decorated the end of the central beam of the pediment of Temple A at Pyrgi. In bronze, there is a series of small statues, dedicated to the gods as offerings in fulfilment of vows, a tradition already

38 Bronze votive statuette from Monteguragazza in Bologna Archaeological Museum

39 *Bronze statuette of a striding warrior*

40 *Stone cinerary urn, carved in the form of an enthroned woman. From Chianciano near Chiusi, and in Florence Archaeological Museum*

begun in the previous century. An example found at Monteguragazza is dated about 470 BC and may be taken to illustrate the style as it developed from the Archaic into an early Classical treatment (*38*). The bronze shows a young man, holding a *phiale* for libation. Although he stands somewhat stiffly, he is seen in a pose with the weight resting on one leg and the other knee thrust forward, while the modelling shows an increased interest in anatomy. Bronzework in relief reached an amazing virtuosity of technique in the Cortona lamp, usually dated to the second half of the fifth century BC, though the overcrowded decoration is in a somewhat doubtful taste (*64*). Meanwhile, elements of older styles were tenaciously retained; the well-known bronze statuettes of striding warriors, sometimes found in Etruria, are now generally considered to be Umbrian, or from districts encircling Umbria. Their elongated proportions recall those of the Geometric style but their military equipment shows they date from the Archaic and on through the Classical period (*39*).

At Chiusi, the long tradition of anthropomorphic urns persisted; a stone example from Chianciano is just under a metre (one yard) in height and has a detached head, which served as a lid. It is carved in the form of a female figure, seated upon a throne and with a child asleep in her lap. The style of the severe but serene face is derived from Classical models of the fifth century BC and shows little concern to describe the features of an individual person (*40*).

It would be easy to believe that the Etruscans did not generally share the contemporary interest of the Greeks in an often somewhat impersonal idealization of the human body; at any rate, there is some evidence for a greater artistic activity in the late Classical style, which lasted down to about 300 BC in Etruria, and which reflects a trend towards a graceful rendering with a less formal and softer modelling. A splendid example of this style is the Mars of Todi, dating to early in the fourth century BC, one of the few large-scale Etruscan bronze statues to survive and which is now in the Vatican Museum. The nearly life-size figure is that of a young warrior, wearing a tunic and corslet, who stands in a well-balanced pose, his left arm lifted to grasp a spear, while he probably held a libation bowl in his right hand. His head, now lacking a helmet, is turned to the right and his expression is one of deep seriousness. A similar sentiment appears on the face of a youth, whose head forms a bronze *oinochoe*, or jug; this is worked in a very fine repoussé technique, with chased details, and, like many utilitarian Etruscan bronzes, reaches the level of a minor work of art (*41*).

Household furnishings with cast bronze figures have already been mentioned in this context and the engraved bronzes are also outstanding in quality, particularly the mirrors, a series already begun in the sixth century BC (p. 115) and caskets, or *cistae*, whose handles and feet were made of cast bronze, while the lids and sides were decorated with beautiful engravings (*69*). The most celebrated example is the Ficorini *Cista*; the handle is formed of a well-composed group of three graceful figures, Bacchus and two satyrs, standing with their arms resting upon each other's shoulders, while each of the three feet presents a design of three young male figures and the complex illustration engraved on the side shows an adventure of the Argonauts, the drawing derived from a Greek original.

86

41 Bronze oinochoe
or jug

Perhaps the most notable contemporary stone sculpture in
Etruria is that of the effigies and reliefs carved upon sarcophagi,
principally from the region around Tarquinia. A fine example
from Vulci, dating to late fourth or early third century BC, has
a fond married couple lying on the top, clasped in each other's
arms, while the relief at the side shows them as they bid each
other a solemn farewell, a motif which was becoming increasingly frequent at this time. Behind the two central figures stand
their attendants; a male servant holds a parasol over the wife's
head and behind him stand two girls, carrying her casket and
fan. The husband's attendants bear his stool and trumpets,
while at the extreme left and right are a flautist and a lyre-
player (*42*).

The conquests of Alexander spread Greek art throughout the
east Mediterranean area and there it mingled with reciprocal
influences to produce the Hellenistic styles of the successor

87

42 Stone sarcophagus from Vulci, with a farewell scene in bas-relief. In the Museum of Fine Arts Athenaum, Boston

kingdoms. During the final three centuries BC, the power of Rome expanded until it included Greece and, finally, the whole Mediterranean world and it is not surprising that Rome, which had for long received most cultural influences, even Hellenic ones, from her cultivated neighbours, the Etruscans, now reversed the rôles; she was in direct contact with the Greek cities and, as Rome grew in political importance, she also played an increasingly creative part in the art of the Hellenistic world.

As we have seen, the Etruscan cities were now subject-allies of Rome and were slowly becoming assimilated into the Roman way of life; nevertheless in the Hellenistic period they retained a regional identity and some local artistic forms, so that their art may still be called specifically Etruscan until the beginning of the Imperial era. Yet it is true that a common artistic expression may be found throughout the Hellenistic sphere, which liked to portray emotion and the dramatic moment and had a taste for individuality and for elegance, all attitudes which appealed to the Etruscans. Perhaps these qualities are most clearly shown in the series of Hellenistic temple terracottas from Etruria. The beautiful winged horses from the pediment of a temple at Tarquinia are not closely dated but show a refined grace (*43*). The terracottas found at Cività Alba depict some rugged Gauls in full flight from the vengeance of Apollo at

Delphi, dropping their loot as they run, and Bacchus in the act of surprising the sleeping Ariadne, scenes which exemplify both the sentiment and the style. The modelling of the bodies, now with the female figures shown nude as well as those of the men, achieves an elegance also found in the contemporary bronzes, with their small beautifully coiffured heads set upon slender bodies, which are turned in supple and languid poses.

If one main current dominated the art of the Hellenistic world, local manifestations continued to be produced in Etruria down to the first century BC, as is shown by the long series of carved sarcophagi or the cinerary chests of stone or terracotta from Volterra, Chiusi or Perugia. The reliefs on these monuments have a new range of subject matter, in which the former joy has largely abandoned the Etruscans and there are repeated sad scenes of farewell, as the dead set out on their

43 Terracotta winged horses from the pediment of a temple at Tarquinia. In Tarquinia Archaeological Museum

journey to the underworld. Mythological events are also constantly repeated and some may suggest a taste for violence and bloodshed.

Many of the figures on these sarcophagi and cinerary chests are true portraits and one cannot leave a discussion of Etruscan sculpture without considering this art form. It is not now generally believed that the Etruscans played a vital part in the creation of the Roman style of portraiture but it is certain that they fully shared the widespread taste for this genre in the final centuries BC; there are many Etruscan heads of this period, either of bronze, terracotta or stone, which show a deep preoccupation in expressing the character of the individual, some of which even approach the imagery of a caricature. Among the most impressive portraits is the life-size statue in bronze, found near Cortona, which is usually called the 'Orator' (*44*). This

44 Bronze statue, called the 'Orator', found near Cortona and now in Florence Archaeological Museum

magnificent work probably dates to the first half of the first century BC and shows a dignified man, dressed in a toga, possibly in the act of addressing an assembly. He is almost indistinguishable from a contemporary Roman gentleman and looks forward into the Romanized world but on the hem of his toga an inscription giving his name, *Aule Meteli*, is written in Etruscan.

PAINTING

The first point to note about the Etruscan paintings is that they have survived at all. They form the only large group of monumental painting from the classical world until that of the Romans and we owe this to the Etruscan custom of painting the walls of some of their rock-cut tombs in fresco. The art form is, of course, closely allied to that of vase painting; huge quantities of Greek painted pottery were imported into Etruria and the several styles of this ware often had a decisive effect upon that of the large-scale paintings. The Etruscans were not alone in practising painting on a large scale. We have descriptions of beautiful Greek works, painted on the walls of public buildings and other media vulnerable to time, so that they have almost all vanished, as have the paintings with which the Etruscans decorated their temples and, perhaps, their houses.†

The custom of tomb painting was confined to comparatively few of the cities; the earliest examples have been found at Veii and Cerveteri but Tarquinia was for long the greatest centre of tomb painting, particularly in the Archaic period, while fifth century examples are known at Chiusi and other scattered sites and the paintings from later tombs at Orvieto and Vulci will be described. With the obvious exception of the supernatural elements, there is little need to doubt that the paintings give a mainly accurate picture of contemporary life and, with some reservations, we may use the paintings as a primary source of information for the details of Etruscan activities.

A small tomb at Veii, discovered in 1958, shows that tomb painting was already practised by the seventh century BC. The lower half of the walls of the Tomb of the Ducks is painted in red and the upper half in yellow; where the colours meet, there are bands of black, yellow and red, on which strut a row of birds

45 Painted frieze from the Tomb of the Ducks, Veii

(*45*). These birds are painted in the same three colours and the vigorous style is borrowed from that of Subgeometric vase painting. In the Campana Tomb, also at Veii, the panels at either side of the door leading into the inner chamber were painted (*14*); the design still has elements of an Orientalizing style. In one scene, a boy is shown perched on a long-legged horse, led by a man, while animals and fabulous beasts vie for space in an entangling floral motif. Here, proportion is largely disregarded and the colours are used quite arbitrarily but, even by the middle of the sixth century, some artists had turned to a more naturalistic style. The Boccanera plaques, a set of five terracotta slabs found at Cerveteri and now in the British Museum, depict a sphinx but also, be they gods or men, some stiff but lifelike figures, painted in black, yellow and a rich brown/purple. A somewhat later set of plaques in the Louvre, called the Campana group, show what is probably a mytho-logical scene and some very real dignitaries, one seated upon a stool in front of an effigy of a goddesss (*102*).

The painted tombs of Tarquinia are rock-cut chambers, many with internal architectural features picked out in colour, though some are painted to represent a tent or pavilion, set up in the open air. Most of the paintings are executed in a fresco technique; the walls were smoothed and covered with a thin coat of plaster, on which the artist first sketched his design, either with a sharp point or outlined in paint, and then, while the plaster was still wet, holding the dampness of the rock walls, he filled in the outline with a wash of uniform paint and added a few details. The early frescos are drawn with the heads in profile, the shoulders often in frontal view and the legs again in profile; the charming effect relies mainly on the drawing of the lines and the inter-relation of the figures, while the bright

46 Achilles in ambush at the fountain, a scene from the Tomb of the Bulls, Tarquinia

93

47 Mourning figures from the Tomb of the Augurs, Tarquinia

colours help to express the sentiment and animation of the
scenes.

The series begins with the Tomb of the Bulls (*46*); only the
end wall, facing the entrance, is painted and, below the gable
are shown two bulls, one with a human face, and two of the
rare erotic scenes from Etruscan art. Below, the main panel
presents a story taken from Greek epic, the only example
known in Archaic painting and undoubtedly taken from a
Greek vase painting. Crouched behind a fountain, Achilles
lies in wait for Troilus, the young son of Priam of Troy, who,
unaware of his fate, rides up to water his horse. The scene
abounds in floral decoration and the details of the fountain,
the water gushing from a lion's mouth into a bronze bowl, are
shown; the style, with plump figures and the long shape of the
skull, indicates the influence of Ionian art.

This tomb is usually dated about 540–530 BC and from this
time to the end of the Archaic period, many delightful pictures
were painted in the tombs of Tarquinia, their themes usually
taken from the funerary rites, banquets or ritual games, though
everyday pleasures were also shown. The Tomb of the Augurs,

dated about 530–520 BC, was decorated on both the end and
the side walls (*47* and *106*). Two mourning figures flank a
doorway painted on the end wall, whilst along the side walls
funerary games were depicted, including a wrestling match
between contestants, whose bulky figures recall those of the
contemporary black-figure vase painting (*58*). The Tomb of the
Painted Vases may show a scene of domestic felicity (p. 177 and
108) and the Tomb of Hunting and Fishing, usually dated
520–510 BC, introduces a joyous illustration of out-of-doors
life, in which a group of boys pursue seaside sports (*107*); this
tomb is painted in a wide range of colours including black,
yellow, red, white, blue and green. This note of exuberant
activity is also found in some representations of funerary games,
like those of the Tomb of the Jugglers at Tarquinia (*48*). In
contrast to this gay atmosphere, the paintings of the Tomb of
the Baron, dating about 510–500 BC, may be mentioned; here,
a calm serenity is felt in the tranquil attitudes of greeting or
worship of the figures, which are among the most delicate of the
Archaic paintings in Etruria.

As in the field of sculpture, there are fewer paintings of the
early Classical style, which often retain Archaic elements well
into the fifth century BC. A good example is that of the Tomb of
the Monkey at Chiusi, where tomb painting had now begun.

48 Entertainers performing, a scene from the Tomb of the Jugglers, Tarquinia

The figures of the athletes recall Archaic forms, though the tomb probably dates to the second quarter of the century. The atmosphere and subject-matter of the paintings remain largely unchanged and banquets and funerary games are shown (*105*). The drawing, however, often shows the influence of the severe Classical style of Greece, best known from the red-figure vase painting of the same date, which developed a new refinement in the design.

One of the most beautiful tomb paintings of this period is that of the Tomb of the Triclinium, dated about 470 BC. Two horsemen flank the doorway and, opposite, the three banqueting couches are shown on the end wall. On either side-wall there are painted five dancers or musicians, men and women alternating, and divided by trees or flowering shrubs, on which perch gaily coloured birds. The gestures of these figures are carefully balanced, their energetic movements are graceful and emphasized by their flying draperies, whose colours, too, are used to integrate the whole fine composition (*49*).

The paintings of the late Classical style of the fourth century BC show a change of mood, subject-matter and technique,

49 A dancer and lyre player from the Tomb of the Triclinium, Tarquinia

50 Head of a woman of the Velcha *family, from the Tomb of Orcus, Tarquinia*

which, though it had been tentatively used in the previous century, is now handled with a new mastery. Like the contemporary vase painting and metal engraving, the drawing demonstrates a greatly increased ability to explore perspective. The figures are shown in well-designed and overlapping groups, conceived in depth, and with poses in three-quarter view or using a strong foreshortening, all of which are drawn with great assurance. In the painting, these effects are heightened by the use of graduated colour, highlights and a careful treatment of light and dark areas; some of these innovations may be seen in the paintings from the Golini Tomb (*93*), in which the scenes include a journey into the underworld and a banquet there.

The mood of the paintings now begins to lose its gaiety and a deep melancholy prevails. This new feeling is caught in the wistful gaze of the beautiful woman of the *Velcha* family, painted in the earlier chamber of the Tomb of Orcus during the fourth century BC (*50*) and it is no coincidence that in the second chamber, painted during the following century, the scenes show a banquet in the underworld, in which demons appear. The mood continued through the Hellenistic period and now, perhaps, one might speak of a sense of foreboding, not only for individuals, but for the Etruscan race. The subjects selected for the paintings of the François Tomb, probably dating to the second or early first century BC, included a violent episode in the ancient, but more successful history of Vulci (p. 27, and

51 Fighting warriors from the François Tomb, Vulci; paintings now in the Torlonia Museum, Rome

51); Achilles' bloody sacrifice of the Trojan prisoners, with the grim figure of *Charun* standing near by; the death struggle of Eteocles and Polynices and a full-length portrait of *Vel Saties*, dressed in elegant robes, who watches a dwarf release a bird, an anxious scene of augury (*103*).

Finally, mention should be made of the Tomb of the Typhon at Tarquinia, among the last tombs to be painted there. The torso of the Typhon, dramatically straining under a great weight, is a fine example of Hellenistic treatment and is painted with virtuosity, while the grouping of a procession of figures in the underworld has been likened to the reliefs of the *Ara Pacis* of Augustus.

Having reached the sophisticated achievements of the Hellenistic period in architecture, sculpture and painting, it is something of a shock to recall the first Etruscan attempts at representational art during the seventh century BC. In these seven hundred years, their art had evolved through an extraordinary spectrum of styles, each the expression of an age. From this background of the major arts, we may now examine the wealth of small objects, often no less aesthetically valuable. We know where some of these objects were found and thus have a guide to their usage and date. But the majority have no recorded provenance and we must rely upon their form and style, closely allied to that of the major arts, to identify them and set them in their correct place in time and thus use them to illustrate the everyday life of the age.

6

Household goods and personal possessions

The houses and tombs already described clearly belonged to people able to afford the luxuries of life. It is, of course, not uncommon to find that such people have left to posterity more monumental witness of their life and death than have the poor and this is especially true of the Etruscans. The division between the classes was marked and we have far more evidence for the lives of the rich, whose tombs have provided most of the objects to be described in this chapter. Down the centuries they display the good taste of the Etruscan nobility, who not only collected objects of exotic worth but also showed a fine appreciation of the work of Greek craftsmen, which, in turn, stimulated the Etruscan potters and smiths to rival their achievements.

POTTERY

Several types of Greek pottery have already been mentioned as articles of trade and a source of inspiration for Etruscan art and these imports were also copied by the Etruscans in ceramic forms, which would be worth studying for this aspect alone. The study of pottery is, however, one of the fundamental disciplines of the archaeologist: unlike many materials, pottery cannot be reused and, though it is breakable, it is nearly indestructible, so that it is found in most archaeological contexts. Moreover the rapid changes in taste, form and technique make it a vital yardstick of chronology, while adding to our aesthetic knowledge.

The Etruscans used various types of vase for differing purposes, often adapting Greek forms, and it will be best to begin by introducing their names and mentioning their most frequent, though not exclusive, usage (*52*). The small *aryballos* and *alabastron* with their narrow necks, were used to hold perfume and toilet oil; the *skyphos, kylix, kantharos* and *rhyton* and some other forms were all drinking cups; the *oinochoe*, the most common form of jug, was frequently used for serving wine and made in various forms with a round, trefoil or beaked lip. The *hydria* was a water jar, equipped with a high handle used for

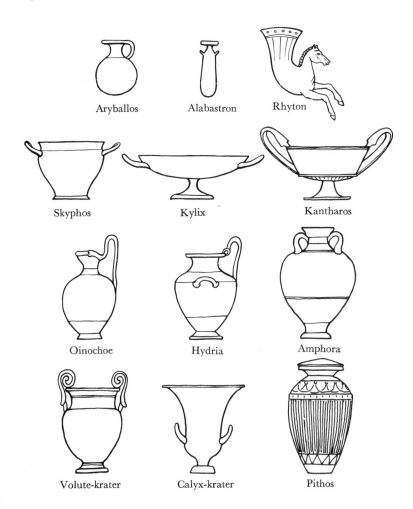

Aryballos   Alabastron   Rhyton

Skyphos   Kylix   Kantharos

Oinochoe   Hydria   Amphora

Volute-krater   Calyx-krater   Pithos

52 Pottery forms and their names; not to scale nor all of the same date

dipping and two carrying handles set on the body; *amphora* is a rather general term used for storage and transportation vessels but, in fine ware, the form was also used as a decanter and was a part of the wine service. The *krater* was used for the mixing of wine and water, as was usual at meals, and, though made in varying forms, always had a wide mouth. The large *pithos* was a storage vessel for liquids, grain and other goods. Finally, the *phiale* was a shallow saucer, often with a hollow boss at the centre of the base, which was frequently used for pouring libations.

The shapes of all these types of vase altered down the centuries, as did their techniques of manufacture and artistic styles. Here, the pottery of fine quality will be mainly discussed but it should be remembered that coarse wares were made and widely used and that pottery served a multitude of purposes, such as reels, weights, boxes, plates, washing bowls, stands, mortars, braziers, footstools, and, as we have seen, was used for objects as large as well heads.

The Villanovans made their ordinary pottery of a fabric frequently called *impasto*, an ill-defined term used to describe Italic wares of impure clay often fired brown/black. In the course of the eighth century BC, however, they also began to copy imported Greek Geometric pottery, imitating the light-coloured ground and decorating it in red/brown paint with designs derived from the Greek style. Traditional Villanovan forms were treated in this manner but new shapes were also introduced, among them copies of Greek cups, *oinochoai* and *kraters*, all forms associated with wine drinking. Euboean influence is discernible in some of this pottery and, by about 700 BC, it is likely that Greek potters, presumably arriving from the settlements on Ischia or at Cuma, were working in Etruria. At this time, Corinthian pottery was beginning to be imported in some quantity and, gradually, the contemporary Orientalizing motifs of the Protocorinthian style were also incorporated into the designs of the local painted wares.

An example of a mingling of a local form with the new motifs may be seen in the strange vessel from Narce in the territory of the Faliscans (near modern Calcata, *53*); the form is based on that of a Villanovan urn, whilst the painted decoration introduces the 'Phoenician' palmette, incidentally drawn

53 Painted urn from Narce in the Pennsylvania University Museum, Philadelphia

up-side-down, and animals. Similar animals, together with birds, fabulous beasts and human figures, also appear on the contemporary incised *impasto*; a refined type of this local ware continued to be made in the seventh century BC, either copying traditional Villanovan shapes or adopting Greek ones (*54A*, two pots on the right).

Before the middle of the seventh century BC, true *bucchero* had evolved; this name is given to a distinctive glossy, black fabric, the principal ceramic speciality of the Etruscans. It was made by burnishing the pot before firing it in a kiln with a restricted supply of oxygen, so that the oxide of iron in the clay turned to black ferrous oxide. Early *bucchero* has thin walls and is frequently decorated with incised lines and dots, much in the tradition of the *impasto* ware described above, but introducing evermore Orientalizing motifs and, sometimes, inscribed with the alphabet (*54B*, three pots on left).

The forms of this type of pottery are very diverse; it will be recalled that at this time the craftsmen of Etruria were seeking inspiration from a wide variety of objects. The potters fully

54A Impasto 'amphoretta' *of the Villanovan tradition and* skyphos.
B *Thin* bucchero *cups and* oinochoe

55A Bucchero *jug with modelled and impressed decoration.* B *Heavy*
bucchero oinochoe

shared this characteristic, following not only traditional and imported pottery forms but also copying ivories and metalwork, including elements modelled as animals or human figures. Impressed decoration was also used, often by means of a roller stamp, producing a repeating pattern; a favourite motif was a procession of animals or men and this style is also found on the coarse ware *pithoi* and braziers of the period (*55A*). In the second half of the sixth century BC, a heavy moulded type of *bucchero* became fashionable; this style has much in common with the contemporary bronzework but is often over-burdened with decoration and it did not last long into the fifth century BC (*55B*).

We have seen that potters in Etruria were borrowing designs from imported Corinthian wares; they also copied the fabric itself. In the earlier of these Italocorinthian vases, the Etruscan copies come close to their Subgeometric originals but the later examples rarely reached a high competence and often have thin paint and a dull finish. The forms generally imitate their Corinthian models, with animals and occasional mythological

56 Italocorinthian oinochoe *in the Metropolitan Museum of Art, New York, Fletcher Fund (1925)*

57 Caeretan hydria *with a hunting scene in the Museum of Fine Arts, Boston, Colburn Fund*

scenes painted in black, with touches of white and purple, on both light and dark grounds; in the latter technique, especially, incision was greatly used as an outline and for internal details (*56*).

Until the sixth century, pottery was imported mainly from Corinth, but by the middle of the century this near-monopoly had been broken by Attic imports. Subsequently, Athenian styles had a considerable, though not exclusive, influence upon Etruscan black-figure ware.

The so-called Pontic group, probably made at Vulci, is a charming black-figure style, using brilliant touches of red and other colours, whose favourite form is copied from the Attic *neck-amphora* but which also followed *bucchero* shapes. The genesis of this school has been much discussed but, whether the founding craftsmen were Greek or Etruscan, the ware was made in Etruria for Etruscan taste, though Attic influence is considerable and so, to a lesser extent, is that of Corinth and Ionia. On the other hand, it is generally agreed that the craftsman who painted the Caeretan *hydriai*, the majority of which have been found at Cerveteri, was an Ionian Greek, presumably a refugee from the troubled conditions of his homeland. These *hydriai* are superbly balanced vessels, painted in black with touches of white and red/purple areas; a lower frieze is frequently painted with an ivy pattern or alternating lotus and palmette motifs, while a mythological scene fills the main zone (*57*).

The origin of Chalcidian ware is still not finally resolved. This beautiful black-figure pottery has only been found in the west Mediterranean area, chiefly from the Chalcidian colonies and in Etruria, so, as the lettering on the vases is also Chalcidian, both Reggio and Cuma have been suggested as the place of manufacture, or that it is the work of Chalcidian potters, living among the Etruscans. Meanwhile, Attic pottery continued to be imported. Some Athenian workshops even made vases specifically for the Etruscan market, like the *amphorae* of the potter Nikosthenes, which were made and painted in Athens but of a form adapted from *bucchero* for the Etruscan taste.

Few individual painters have been recognized among the other Etruscan black-figure groups, which tend to rely less upon

59 Red-figure skyphos, *painted in Civita Castellana (Falerii Veteres). In the Museum of Fine Arts, Boston, Perkins Collection*

58 Black-figure neck-amphora *in the British Museum*

colour, though white paint and incision were often used. Attic influence is predominant and the painting is vigorous, if seldom refined; the principal scenes are usually of quite graceful animals or sturdy human figures, set in a wide background, with little subsidiary detail. An exuberant quality, already noted in other contemporary art forms, fills these scenes; as Beazley remarked of the Micali painter, he must have enjoyed himself! A black-figure *neck-amphora* by this painter catches this gay atmosphere; a chariot race, sports, acrobatics, dancing and a boxing match are all taking place, while a small boy stands ready with a sponge and oil flask (*58*).

Like other cultural manifestations of the fifth century BC, Etruscan vase painting lagged behind that of Greece and black-figure pottery continued to be produced when the Greeks had generally abandoned it for the red-figure technique. In this form of vase painting, the figures were first outlined on the ground of the vase, some internal details were added and then the background filled in, so that in the final product the figures stand out in red/orange from a black background. The technique permitted a new range of drawing and, from the first half of the fifth century BC, there are a number of Etruscan copies of Greek red-figure vases, which, like the contemporary wall paintings, show an appreciation of the new style of drawing but which are always executed in red paint over a dark ground.

True red-figure technique was not attempted in Etruria until the second half of the fifth century BC, when the vases are often close to their Attic originals but, during the fourth century, several cities were producing red-figure pottery, which now also showed the influence of the south Italian schools. An early centre was probably at Vulci but, about 400 BC, a workshop was started at Civita Castellana (Falerii Veteres) which, at its best, produced vases of a high competence and grace. Like the contemporary wall painting and metal engraving, the drawing shows a new virtuosity and groups of well-integrated figures are shown in a wide ground; the scenes, often on large *kraters*, depict mythological stories, in compositions similar to those known in other art forms, women at their toilets and scenes of farewell, often introducing demons. A *skyphos*, which was painted at Civita Castellana (Falerii Veteres) towards the end of the fourth century BC, has a scene in which a man is bidding farewell to his wife, while a demon stands at her side, ready to lead her to the underworld and the handles are bordered with splendid palmettes (*59*). A less ambitious red-figure ware was produced in northern Etruria, perhaps at Chiusi and certainly at Volterra; this fabric included vases made in the form of human heads or modelled as birds. In the south, a series of plates, with a female head as their main decoration, was made at Civita Castellana (Falerii Veteres) and then at Cerveteri (Caere) and this type, which continued into the third century BC, was among the last of the red-figure fabrics of Etruria.

Painted pottery continued to be made in the third and even the second century BC, sometimes using several colours, but taste changed increasingly to the so-called black-glaze wares. This pottery, covered by a uniform black paint, often imitated metallic shapes and was moulded in high relief, a type well known in Campania. A group of silvered vases, often of very ornate form and also decorated in high relief, is found in the area around Lake Bolsena (*60*). This fabric also dates from the Hellenistic period and is the last important local pottery type of Etruria. However, one should not leave the discussion of the pottery without a reference to a fabric from the region of ancient Etruria, which became famous; it was the potters of Arezzo,

60 Silvered calyx-krater *and* volute-krater *from the district around Lake Bolsena* (*Volsinii*)

who, in the first century BC, began to produce the moulded, red-glaze, Arretine pottery, which was to become favourite Roman table ware in the following centuries.

BRONZES

Etruscan household bronzes were celebrated in antiquity and the Greeks thought they excelled in this form of craftsmanship; Kritias, one of the Thirty Tyrants of Athens at the end of the fifth century BC, after saying that Etruscan gold cups were best, added 'also their bronzes, of every sort for the decoration and service of houses' and Pherecrates, a Greek poet of the fifth century BC, wrote 'the lamp-stand was Etruscan . . . for they were skilled and loving craftsmen'. The long tradition of Etruscan bronzework was indeed excellent: not only did they have the natural resources but they appreciated the beauty of the material, making a wide variety of objects some of which have already been mentioned as minor works of art, enhancing our knowledge of Etruscan sculpture and drawing. Perhaps some of these domestic objects were collected, as well as the *tyrrhena sigilla*, or Etruscan statuettes, which were so avidly sought after by the Romans, as they are today.†

Bronze vessels, especially those used for the serving of wine, often followed Greek forms and are similar to their pottery equivalents and, from time to time, each medium influenced the other. There are illustrations of such vessels, like the huge *krater* painted in the Tomb of the Lionesses at Tarquinia and many actual examples of *amphorae, kraters, hydriai* and *oinochoai,* often with cast bronze figures as decoration, like that of the nude youth which serves as a handle on an *oinochoe,* and was probably made at Vulci (*61A*). Ladles and strainers were habitually made of bronze and are shown, held by serving boys, in many banqueting scenes (*61B, 61C, 37* and *108*). Such ladles have been found in sets of varying size, designed to measure out the wine and water; some are decorated in low relief and the handle ends, curved for suspension, are often modelled as the heads of birds or animals. The strainers may be quite simple or reach the level of minor works of art with finely cast handles, sometimes accompanied by hinged funnels, or with the actual holes, through which the liquid ran, worked into a sophisticated design.

*61*A *Bronze* oinochoe, *probably made at Vulci.* B *Bronze ladle.* C *Bronze strainer*

62 Bronze candelabrum, probably made at Vulci. Found in Bologna, now in Bologna Archaeological Museum

Some types of household bronze furniture have already been mentioned above (pp. 80 and 86). For lighting their houses, the Etruscans used both tallow candles and oil lamps. Tall candelabra, sometimes reaching over a metre and a half (four feet) in height, stood on three feet and were often decorated with human figures placed at the top of the central shaft (*62*); horizontal prongs pierced the candles and held them upright, as is shown in a painting from the Golini Tomb (*72*). The smaller candelabra stood on tables and these often have a figure supporting the central column at the base; a pleasing though eccentric example of Etruscan ingenuity may be seen in a small candelabrum with an expanding top, which rises from the shoulders of a nude serving boy, standing with an *oinochoe* in his hand (63A). The oil lamps needed a fibre wick threaded through a nozzle and tweezers for adjusting these wicks have been found with the lamps; these range from simple forms with one wick to the magnificent bronze Cortona lamp, with six-teen nozzles, which, since it was designed to be suspended from the ceiling, has the elaborate decoration on the under side (64).

A large number of incense-burners also survive; a form with panels between the legs may be seen balanced upon the head of a girl, painted in the Tomb of the Jugglers (48), or set upon a table in the scene from the Golini Tomb (72). Another design, similar to that of the table candelabra, had a central shaft, often supported at the base by human figures. Many of these are a rather generalized type, either beautiful youths or maidens, athletes or dancers, but some seem taken straight from life, like a boy playing with a dog or a woman feeding her swaddled child (63B).

63A *Bronze table candelabrum in Bologna Archaeological Museum.*
B *Bronze incense-burner in Tarquinia Archaeological Museum*

64 The Cortona lamp in the Museo dell'Accademia Etrusca, *Cortona*

Braziers for charcoal fires, which warmed the houses, were made of bronze as well as of terracotta; some are rectangular and set upon wheels, others are round and have handles for lifting. Their equipment included rakes, often ending in the form of a human hand, and tongs; shovels are also known with finely cast handles and they may have been used for carrying

65 Bronze brazier with rakes and tongs in the Vatican Museum, Rome

burning charcoal (*65*). Sets of spits for roasting meat were kept threaded upon decorated handles for suspension and were made of iron as well as of bronze, as may be seen from examples from the Monteleone Tomb, where they were found together with iron fire-dogs and a small grid, probably used for cooking over charcoal (*66*). Among other utilitarian bronzes are the meat-hooks, portable candle-holders, washing basins and their

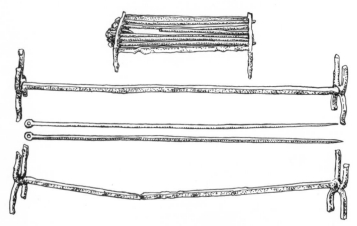

66 Iron spits, fire-dogs and grid from Monteleone, in the Metropolitan Museum of Art, New York

accompanying jugs; further types of fine bronzes include tripod stands, made to support cauldrons, buckets with cast feet and swinging handles, offering bowls, often with beautifully cast handles, stands for the suspension of lamps or vessels and *kottabos* stands, used in a game to be described below (p. 178).

The bronzes used as toilet articles, almost all for women, form an exquisite category of their own. Little has yet been said of the hand mirrors, perhaps the most famous of all Etruscan bronze types; some had hinged cases, decorated in high relief, but usually the discs were attached to cast handles or to tangs, which were sometimes fitted into carved ivory or bone sockets. The face of the disc was polished to a good reflecting surface and, on the back, scenes were presented either in very low relief or, much more often, with engraved lines, an Etruscan speciality. The numerous inscriptions on Etruscan mirrors have proved a valuable source of information for both epigraphists and linguists and the scenes evoke a world of their own; their themes range from stories taken from Greek mythology and Etruscan tales to events, both serious and light-hearted, from everyday life, which deserve much attention. Here, we may see women as they wash themselves at a wide basin, set at waist height on a low pedestal, sometimes with a water jar, a *hydria*, close by or an oil flask and other toilet articles; we may see them as they arrange their hair or put on their jewellery, taken from boxes. The fourth-century mirror illustrated here shows *Turan*, the Etruscan name for Venus, at her toilet (*67*); she is wearing rich contemporary clothes and jewellery and is sitting upon a luxurious cushion, set on a high stool with turned legs. She is gazing into a mirror, held by a winged attendant, while another stands at her side with an *alabastron* in one hand and a perfume pin in the other. These long pins were required to dip into the narrow perfume bottles, for the scent was not always liquid, and they were cast with finely modelled handles (*68A*). An equal elegance is found in the design of some *strigils*, the implements used to scrape the body after anointing it with oil, as was done after exercise or washing; the handle of a bronze *strigil* is cast in the form of a girl, who is herself performing this action (*68B*).

The *cistae*, or caskets, with their cast handles and feet, have already been mentioned as works of art (p. 86); like the mirrors,

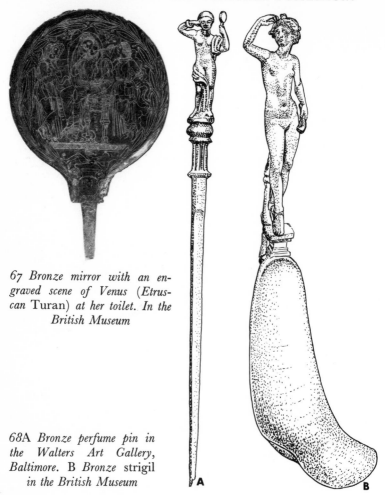

67 *Bronze mirror with an engraved scene of Venus (Etruscan* Turan) *at her toilet. In the British Museum*

68A *Bronze perfume pin in the Walters Art Gallery, Baltimore.* B *Bronze* strigil *in the British Museum*

many were made at Palestrina. Some are rectangular, others are oval with hinged lids but the majority are cylindrical, made to hold personal possessions like a lady's toilet equipment. A reference to this function may, perhaps, be seen in the handle group of a *cista* in the British Museum, in which the woman holds an *alabastron* and the man an oil flask and *strigil* (69).

Delicate toilet articles have actually been found in the *cistae*; one, now in the Boston Museum of Fine Arts, contained a

69 *Bronze* cista *with an engraved scene of Bellerophon and Pegasus. In the British Museum*

70 A, *Glass perfume bottle, wooden boxes and* B, *bronze oil flask*

multicoloured glass perfume bottle, carved wooden boxes with compartments for cosmetics, *spatulae*, a wooden comb and a sponge (*70A*). In other tombs, there have also been found ivory and bone hairpins, bronze nail files and oil flasks of exotic forms (*70B*), as well as small gold and silver boxes. One can imagine such delightful objects as treasured possessions and it is pleasant to recall an inscription on the Ficorini *Cista* in archaic Latin (for the casket was made in Rome though in the Etruscan tradition) which records 'Dindia Macolnia gave me to her daughter'.

OTHER HOUSEHOLD GOODS

The bronzes must have been among the most splendid objects in an Etruscan house and we are fortunate that so many have survived. Many other types of furniture have vanished, since they were made of wood, leather, basketry, cloth or other perishable materials and these we principally know from illustrations of various kinds.

A form of chair, with a high, rounded back, based on a basketry prototype, has been mentioned above (*30*); it was a local form and continued to be used down the centuries. Models from Chiusi, both of backed chairs and four-legged tables, show that wooden frame furniture was also used in the seventh century BC and we may assume it was customary to sit at meals at this time. Influence from the east Mediterranean may be seen in the design of the low bed and high throne, covered with bronze repoussé plaques, found in the Regolini-Galassi Tomb of the seventh century (*71*) but, as with so many aspects of Etruscan life, Greek forms predominated by the sixth century and afterwards Etruscan furniture continued to follow Hellenic models.

The Etruscans, however, used them in their own manner; it was not customary for Greek women to attend banquets with their husbands but, in Etruria, there are frequent banqueting scenes in which both men and women, undoubtedly husband and wife, are shown reclining together on high couches. This is the Greek *kline*, used for sleeping as well as for dining; it is generally shown with a head-board and the legs are often rectangular with incisions and volutes at the top. These couches are covered with deep mattresses, often larger and deeper than

71 Throne from the Regolini-Galassi Tomb, Cerveteri, reconstructed from the evidence of the bronze fittings. In the Vatican Museum, Rome

those of the Greeks, and with cushions, sometimes folded double (*35, 108*). Low tables were placed in front of the banqueting couches; these tables are usually of the three-legged Greek type, with a rectangular top and two legs at one end opposed to one at the other, and occasionally have a lower shelf, on which dishes could be stacked. During the sixth century BC, there are, too, many representations of folding stools, some with carved animal feet or decorated with ivory plaques (p. 164, and *102*); archaeological evidence for such stools is provided by the bronze pivot pins and four sockets for the feet, which have been found in tombs.

The Etruscans do not seem to have used high-backed chairs very often, though some rather grand versions are illustrated, like the throne which forms part of a cinerary urn from near Chiusi (*40*). Footstools, some with claw feet, and stools, shown with elaborated turned legs, were used (*67*) and, during the fourth century BC, the Etruscans also adopted from Greece the high, round-topped tables with three legs, carved in animal

72 A laden side table from the banqueting scene of the Golini Tomb, Orvieto; painting now in Florence Archaeological Museum

73 Interior of the Tomb of the Reliefs, Cerveteri

form, a furniture type shown laden with *kraters* and *oinochoai* in the paintings from the Golini Tomb (*72*). During the Hellenistic period, furniture grew more ornate, even baroque in taste; household bronzes, chairs, tables and stools were all covered with decoration. Women attending banquets are now generally shown seated on chairs, or at the foot of their husband's couch; these couches have appliqué ornamentation and are covered with rich fabrics, woven or embroidered in many colours, or arranged in sophisticated draperies, while the cushions have coloured tassels and fringes.

By modern standards, both Greek and Etruscan interiors were quite sparsely filled; they did not habitually use shelves in their houses nor did they build cupboards and, though they had chests without drawers, they kept many of their possessions either in boxes, baskets or hung on the walls, suspended from hooks or nails. A tomb at Cerveteri marvellously evokes this aspect of an Etruscan interior; it is the Tomb of the Reliefs, dated to the third century BC. It is cut deep into the rock and the outer walls of the chamber have a series of recesses, carved to resemble couches on which lay the dead, while all around them, as if hanging from nails on the walls, are representations of their possessions, moulded in stucco which was painted in many colours (*73*).

Generations of the *Matunas* family were buried in this tomb;

in the middle of the back wall (centre, 73) was the place of honour, which had a woman's name written beside it. This recess was carved to resemble an ornate couch and in front stands a low foot-stool on which a pair of red slippers is laid. To the left is a chest, clearly made of wood, with a door and key-hole, while the pile of neatly folded material shown on the top may indicate that this was a clothes chest. On the pilaster above are shown a jug and a black drinking cup; on the balancing pilaster to the right, there are a fan, coloured wreaths, which were worn at banquets, and a stick. On the frieze above the recesses, the military equipment of the men of the family is presented; one may see their swords, shields, helmets and greaves, while a pair of great, bronze, circular trumpets flank the doorway. On four sides of the central pillars, there is a fascinating display of domestic objects, some quite unfamiliar to us, as they were habitually made of perishable materials, and these have raised much speculation. On the pillar to the left, the facing panel has a wooden baton, hung from a thong, a large knife, an axe, a jug, a coil of rope and what are believed to be slings; on the right side of the same pillar are shown a leather bag with a strap, a decorated drinking bowl, a long stick with a curved end, either comparable to a *lituus* or simply a crooked staff, and an object which has so far baffled certain identification, though a cradle or a wheeled-stand have both recently been suggested. Opposite, on the facing panel of the pillar to the right, one may see a ladle, tongs and a pan, while above is a large tray, suspended from a handle; this object is almost certainly a gaming board, for parallel lines are visible upon the surface and the small purse associated with it would have held the dice or counters. On the adjacent panel to the right, more slings hang from the volutes and next to them is an object which some believe to be a basket, while others have suggested a round cheese. A set of spits is neatly hung from a handle on the right, there is a wooden knife rack, with two knives placed in it, and below a basin is shown upon a tripod, while animals and birds, among them a duck, so often seen in banqueting scenes, fill out the remaining spaces.

LUXURY GOODS AND JEWELLERY

There can be no doubt that the Etruscan nobility liked grandeur

74 *Ivory chalice from Palestrina in the Villa Giulia Museum, Rome*

75 *Gold* fibula *from the Regolini-Galassi Tomb, Cerveteri in the Vatican Museum, Rome*

and took a carefree delight in display; during the centuries of their prosperity, they enjoyed wearing jewellery and used luxury goods made of glass, faience, amber, ivory, precious stones, silver and gold, both imported and made in Etruria.

The Villanovans of the eighth century BC had worn coloured glass beads, trinkets of precious metals and faience pendants, which reached them by trade from the east Mediterranean area, while their own craftsmen produced traditional jewellery. The most important local type, the ever-changing *fibulae*, were made from an astonishing variety of forms; they were usually made of bronze, though there are examples in gold, silver or iron, which was still considered to have some rarity value, and these *fibulae* were decorated with bone, amber and, occasionally, glass-paste.

The extraordinary wealth of Etruria during the Orientalizing period of the seventh century BC brought not only an influx of exotic objects but also a very rapid development of Etruscan jewellery and luxury objects. The Bocchoris Tomb, dated about 675 BC, is named from a coloured faience vase, decorated with Egyptian motifs including the cartouche of that Pharaoh. Silver and silver-gilt bowls were imported from a Phoenician source and their repoussé and engraved scenes of war and peace were imitated in Etruria. Ivory was imported and carved, some probably by craftsmen from the east Mediterranean working in Etruria; the forms include boxes and chalices, carved in relief or with figures in the round (74). Other exotic imports were the magnificent bronzes, carved tridacna shell from the Red Sea and painted ostrich eggs, sometimes found together with alabaster jars and scarabs.

The contemporary jewellery was of an equal richness and was mainly made in Etruria, whose goldsmiths incorporated Orientalizing designs into their work and reached an amazing virtuosity of technique, using repoussé, filigree and, above all, granulation, a method of decoration in which very small, spherical grains of gold are soldered onto a background to form a pattern. The jewellery worn by individuals must have reached an almost barbaric splendour; a good example is that of the lady *Larthia*, buried in the inner chamber of the Regolini-Galassi Tomb, whose name was written on some of her most precious possessions. She was laid in the tomb wearing on her breast a huge gold pectoral, decorated with zones of animals in repoussé work and with gold ear-rings and a cloak-clasp, similar to those worn by the terracotta figures from Cerveteri (*31*). One of her golden *fibulae* was no less than thirty-one centimetres (one foot) in length; on the back there originally stood fifty-two birds, modelled in gold sheet and with details picked out in granulation, while lions were depicted in repoussé on the plate (*75*). Among the other jewellery from this tomb, there are over twenty *fibulae* with long catch-plates, a double necklace of plaited gold wire from which hung pendants, some of amber set in gold, finger-rings, bracelets and a number of small plaques of thin gold sheet, which had been sewn onto cloth. In addition, jewellery dating to the seventh century BC includes pins, with their heads beautifully decorated in granulation, buckles and hair-bands.

During the Archaic period, jewellery became less ostentatious and much of it was influenced by current Greek styles,

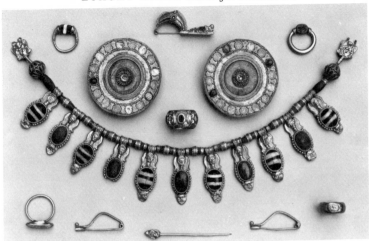

76 Archaic jewellery from Vulci in the Metropolitan Museum of Art, New York, Harris Brisbane Dick Fund (1940)

notably those of Ionia. The series of Italic *fibulae* persisted, however, many with a long catch-plate with a knob or an animal perched at the end (*76*). *Baule* ear-rings, shaped like tiny carrying-bags, became fashionable, as did disc ear-rings, a design adopted from the Greek world. Jewellery was now often inlaid with semi-precious stones or coloured glass; gold finger-rings were worn, decorated either in relief or with engraved patterns and, at this time, attractive gems were cut in Etruria, some probably by immigrant Greek craftsmen and were used as jewellery, rather than as seals (*76*).

Among the outstanding luxury goods of the sixth century BC are some finely carved amber and ivories, some purely decorative but others utilitarian, like panelled boxes or carved combs (*78*). There are examples of charming little perfume bottles made of coloured glass and equipped with tiny gold stands, to hold them upright. Gold and silver cups and jugs had already been made in Etruria during the previous century, following east Mediterranean and Greek models, but amongst the finest of all the surviving Etruscan gold cups is an example covered with granulated decoration, which is usually dated to the sixth century BC (*77*). This must be one of those Etruscan golden bowls, a type so admired by Kritias and, though we do not

77 Gold bowl with granulated decoration in the Victoria and Albert Museum, London

have many later examples, it should be recalled that Diodorus records that the Etruscans used many silver cups at their banquets.

Hollow pendants were frequently worn as amulets by the Etruscans, either hung from necklaces, or we may see them bound to the upper arm or forehead (*41*); they were worn by children and animals, as well as adults. The custom of wearing

78 Carved ivory comb in the Walters Art Gallery, Baltimore

79 Terracotta sarcophagus from Chiusi, showing jewellery worn in the Hellenistic period. In the British Museum

the *bulla aurea* or *Etruscum aurum* was adopted at Rome, especially for generals as they celebrated their triumph and for boys of good family, until they came of age. There are many examples of *bullae* from Etruria. Some are of gold, worked in fine repoussé, like the interesting example of the early Classical period, now in the Walters Art Gallery, Baltimore, which shows Daedalus and Icarus with their distinctive tools.

A number of wreaths, with realistic leaves cut from thin gold sheet, are known from the Classical period and later and, during the fourth century, ear-rings tended to become very large, often with little decoration but relying for their effect upon the convex surfaces of the thin gold. Though the fashion for wearing torques, or metal neck-bands, must have come from a Gaulish source, Etruscan ladies of the Hellenistic period generally followed Greek types of jewellery, as may be seen from that worn by *Seianti Thanunia Tlesnasa*, as she reclines upon a sarcophagus, dated to the second century BC (*79*). She wears a tiara upon her head and small ear-rings with coloured pendants, as well as disc brooches at her shoulders, bracelets and finger-rings. The mirrors and *strigils* used by Etruscan ladies of the late Classical and Hellenistic period for their toilet were sometimes made of silver.

CLOTHES AND HAIR-STYLES

The clothes worn by the Etruscans were generally made from material woven of wool or flax and were of the loose, draped forms common in the ancient Mediterranean world. There is almost no direct evidence for these perishable objects but we have a few references in the ancient sources and they are well documented in the representational arts, though these tell us little before the seventh century BC. At this time, women are shown wearing tunics, usually belted, which reach down to their ankles and some also have rectangular cloaks, fastened at the shoulders; their hair was worn in a long braid, which fell down their backs. The men were clean shaven and their hair is often seen drawn back from the forehead to reach the nape of the neck at the back; they, too, are shown wearing long tunics, sometimes decorated with a chequered pattern.

The evidence from the sixth century BC is wider and shows that fashions had become much more Hellenic; the men sometimes follow the Greek semi-nudity, only wearing a loin-cloth or a cloak wrapped around their hips, a custom which continued in later centuries, but only athletes and serving boys are habitually shown naked. The men either wear a long tunic reaching to their ankles or, like the boys, a short close-fitting tunic with short sleeves, which may be white or coloured and sometimes has a border. Over the tunics, they may wear a very short cloak, whose ends are thrown over the left shoulder but which passes under the right arm, leaving it free; there are examples both in purple and with a border (*102*). This small cloak is believed to be the original type for the *trabea*, worn at Rome by the older colleges of priests and by the knights on ceremonial occasions, but, even by the sixth century BC, the cloaks worn by the Etruscans had developed into a longer form, reaching down to the knees, like those worn by the mourners in the Tomb of the Augurs (*47*). This type of cloak may already be termed the *tebenna*, the type of cloak associated with the Etruscans, which, like the toga was cut from the segment of a circle and may be seen with the hem rising on the left side.†

At this time, men wore their hair long, often with a few coils falling forward over their shoulders and they are usually shown with beards.

Both men and women had gaily coloured scarves, or shawls, either flung over their arms or shoulders, or tied at the waist, the ends flying behind them as they danced. The women continued to wear a long tunic with short sleeves, sometimes with borders and they were still shown in rectangular cloaks, some with slits for the arms, which they also occasionally pulled up over their heads. Their hair was dressed in long ringlets, some falling forward over their shoulders, or lying free upon their backs; sometimes they had a head-band across their foreheads, from which peeped a neat row of curls. In the second half of the sixth century, they adopted a high, domed type of hat, called the *tutulus*, but generally the Etruscans did not cover their heads, though the colonists in the Po Valley are frequently shown wearing broad-brimmed hats. From Ionia, too, came shoes with turned up toes, the *calcei repandi*, which were worn by both sexes and are shown in the paintings with both black or coloured leather. Some examples reach half-way up the calf and are tied with thongs (*102*) but others are light and laced up

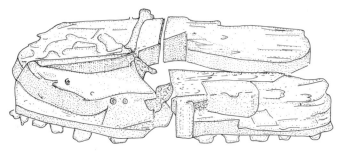

80 Pair of hinged sandal soles of bronze

the front, like those worn by the lady on the sarcophagus from Cerveteri (*35*). Etruscan shoes and sandals were famous in antiquity and examples of hinged sandals, made of wood and with bronze soles, have actually survived (*80*).

In early Classical times, it became fashionable for men to cut their hair short and beards became quite rare; the *tebenna* grew longer, covering the knee, and was brilliantly coloured. Decorated shawls are shown, worn even by slaves. Women's hair-styles became shorter, rarely reaching below their ears and were often arranged in curls upon their cheek (*50*); some contemporary paintings show women with conspicuously fair hair, so that there is the suspicion that they used bleach. Women now habitually wore cloaks similar to those of the men and light, full tunics, which, in the Hellenistic style, were frequently without sleeves and belted high above the waist. During this period, they dressed their hair in a number of elegant ways, like that with the hair piled high upon the head and held with bands, which may be seen on a contemporary flask (*70*).

Men still wore their hair short and beards virtually disappeared; the *tebenna* became even longer, almost reaching the ankles, much more voluminous and often white. In the third century paintings of the Tomb of the Shields at Tarquinia, the musicians wear long, white cloaks but those of the members of the *Velcha* family have red or black borders. In the François Tomb, the struggling warriors wear tunics with borders at the hem and across the shoulders (*51*), while the figure of *Vel Saties* is wrapped in a purple cloak. By this time, the Etruscans were becoming increasingly absorbed into the Roman way of life and it is in tune with the times that *Aule Meteli*, the Orator, should wear a toga and also the high, leather boots tied with four thongs, a form which not only goes back to Etruscan prototypes of the sixth century BC, but which was one of the special pieces of apparel of a Roman senator (*44*).

7

War, trade, industry and agriculture

WAR

There are few written records which help us understand the Etruscans' organization in war, nor do the representations of battle scenes allow us to visualize their tactics down the centuries. It is best to preface a description of what we know of their military and naval methods by an account of the tangible evidence of their arms and armour.

By the eighth century BC, the Villanovans were well armed with short swords and fine spears, still often made of bronze. They had excellent defensive equipment, chiefly the crested helmets, corslets and round shields. The shields were held by a single, central handle and were decorated with geometric designs or, after the advent of Orientalizing motifs, with zones of animals (4, 5B).

During the following centuries armour continued to be made of bronze, but by the seventh century BC weapons were usually of iron and, from this moment onwards, far fewer examples survive. This lack of direct evidence is, however, compensated for by a greatly increased number of representations of fully equipped warriors. But some of these contemporary illustrations, like that on the central panel of the Monteleone chariot, show not the arms and armour of the period but demonstrate their artistic borrowings, ultimately based upon mythological sources.

By about the middle of the seventh century BC, the old Villanovan forms were beginning to be replaced by Greek types, though these were not all adopted at the same time. This new Greek equipment included the beautiful Corinthian type of helmet, whose dome, deep neck protection, cheek-pieces and noseguard were all hammered from a single piece of bronze

81 Stele of Avele Feluske *from Vetulonia in Florence Archaeological Museum*

and which was fitted with either a low or a stilted crest. Secondly, the Etruscans adopted a Greek type of greave, which clipped onto the leg below the knee and, thirdly, the great circular hoplite shield, which was held both by an arm band and a handle, set at the flat rim, and whose slightly convex surface was often decorated with an identifying blazon. These Greek types of military equipment are worn by *Avele Feluske*, whose figure is incised upon a *stele* from Vetulonia, dated about the end of the seventh century BC, though he holds in his hand a double-axe, probably a symbol of authority *(81)*. The same equipment is often shown worn by warriors of the sixth century BC, together with a 'bell' corslet, so-called from the shape of the two bronze plates covering the chest and back down to the waist and with a short sword and either throwing or thrusting spears.

Towards the end of the Archaic age some innovations appear, including a new form of corslet, which could be made of leather, though it is often shown overlaid with lamellated scales

132

or bands, probably made of metal. This composite type of corslet was fastened in front and had shoulder-pieces, attached at the back and laced on the chest, while a series of flaps covered the hips. A variant type of Corinthian helmet was also used, designed with spaces left open for the ears and emphasizing the ridge over the forehead and round the dome; the kneeling warrior from among the temple terracottas of Civita Castellana (Falerii Veteres) is protected by these types, as well as wearing greaves and thigh-guards (*82*).

All this equipment was derived from the Greek world but the Etruscans also sometimes used Italic forms. A fine warrior painted upon a plaque from Cerveteri has a round disc strapped to his chest, a form of heart-guard used by Picene and Samnite warriors, while the famous Etruscan helmet, captured by the Syracuscans in the sea battle off Cuma in 474 BC and dedicated at Olympia (*10*), is of a type also used by the eastern and northern neighbours of the Etruscans and may be seen worn by marching soldiers on the Certosa *situla*. This celebrated bronze

82 Terracotta temple decoration from Civita Castellana, showing warriors fighting. In the Villa Giulia Museum, Rome

bucket is decorated with a series of scenes, including groups of spearmen equipped in three differing manners; the bucket was found in a cemetery at Bologna dating to the period of Etruscan colonization but the *situla* type is Venetic and we cannot be confident that either the arms and armour or the division into three ranks should be considered as evidence for Etruscan practice.

During the fifth century BC, there are many representations of warriors wearing crested helmets with hinged cheek-pieces, without a nose-guard and with a firm frontlet across the brow, and this Attic type of helmet continued to be worn in the fourth century, together with the composite corslet, greaves and the hoplite shield. Another type of corslet was also used; it was made of either bronze or leather and was made to fit the muscles of the abdomen, while at the base it covered the stomach but rose at the sides to leave the hips free, though these were protected by a series of flaps. A fine muscle corslet of bronze, with the front and back plates hinged at the shoulders, was found in a fourth-century tomb at Orvieto, together with a large circular shield, still with some traces of the original wooden backing, and a pair of greaves. This equipment was all in the Greek tradition but it was associated with a type of helmet entirely different from those described above (*83*).

This helmet has a knob at the top of the dome and cheek-pieces decorated with three discs; the rim is almost horizontal but for a slight brim, worn at the back to protect the neck. Both Gaulish and Italic peoples used such helmets and, by the fourth century BC, such reciprocal borrowing had become quite common, though it is not always clear where the types originated. A form of shield, oval in shape and defined by a long central boss which is often associated with the Gauls, like the naked warrior shown fighting a mounted Etruscan on a bas-relief at Bologna, may have had Italic prototypes (*84*). On the other hand, the Etruscans and their Italic neighbours adopted Gaulish types of equipment, including a form of sword seen on the walls of the Tomb of the Reliefs at Cerveteri. This Gaulish element was the last major contribution to Etruscan military equipment before the city-states submitted to Rome and their fighting forces were incorporated into the Roman system.

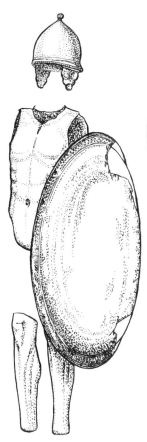

83 Helmet and armour from a tomb at Orvieto, in Florence Archaeological Museum

84 Stele with bas-relief showing a mounted Etruscan fighting a Gaul, in Bologna Archaeological Museum

The Etruscans were credited in antiquity with the invention of the bronze war trumpet, which was used at Rome by the sixth century BC and was already famous in Greece by the beginning of the Classical period.† There are many Etruscan illustrations of such trumpets, usually shown in military processions or funerary scenes; there were several types but two appear most often. One has a straight pipe with a sharply turned end and flaring mouth; the second is of the type seen on the walls of the Tomb of the Reliefs, with a pipe forming an almost complete

circle. Both these forms are carried by the attendants seen on the
side of the sarcophagus from Vulci (*42*).

Though naturally not only used as military equipment, horse-
gear may be mentioned here. In the seventh century BC, the
Etruscans still sometimes used a developed form of the bronze
horse-bits with cheek-pieces modelled as horses, which had
been adopted by the Villanovans (*6A*). Soon, however, a Greek
form with a semicircular cheek piece was accepted and this
type remained in use until the Hellenistic period (*43*). We have
seen that very elaborate chariots were made in Etruria during
the sixth century BC. It is doubtful if chariots were ever used
by the Etruscans in military engagements but, to judge from
the artistic representations, kings or generals did ride to war in
them and certainly the chariot played an important part in
victory processions. Mounted soldiers are also seen in the art
of this period but they wear the heavy equipment of infantrymen and it has been suggested, even though Livy does mention
cavalry engagements during the regal period at Rome, that
such horsemen dismounted to fight and were principally used
as mobile reinforcements, though there may have been true
cavalry as well.

Such difficulties and discrepancies in our evidence indicate
the hazards in attempting to suggest how Etruscan armies were
organized and how they fought in battle, during the crucial
struggles of the Archaic and Classical period. The battle scenes
we possess are not explicit, though there are representations
of marching warriors, armed as heavy infantrymen in the full
Greek equipment, and of single combats. One scene shown in
bas-relief on a sarcophagus in Perugia vividly illustrates a victorious band, returning from a raid. In front walk the roped
prisoners, one carrying a *situla* of Venetic form, followed by
pack mules, loaded with spoils, and led by a figure with a goad
in his hand, while others herd some captured goats and cattle
(*85*).

We may also catch glimpses of warlike scenes from the
ancient sources. There is the description of Porsenna's camp
or that of the successful Etruscan ambush of the Fabian clan
near the banks of the Cremera in about 477 BC, when they are
said to have harassed the Romans with javelins, slings, and
arrows. Again, we hear of the death of Lars Tolumnius, king of

85 Stone sarcophagus with a bas-relief showing the return from a raid. In Perugia Archaeological Museum

Veii (who was incidentally wearing a linen corslet at the time), at the hands of the Roman Consul. There is a description of the battle fought between the men of Chiusi and a Gaulish horde, when the Roman ambassadors are said to have joined the Etruscan battle-line and one of them, riding out in front, killed the Gaulish leader as he charged the Etruscan standards. According to a strange account of a battle in the war between Tarquinia and Rome during the fourth century BC the Etruscans engaged in battle with 'their priests, bearing serpents and torches before them' and 'came rushing on like furies'. Yet much in all these descriptions may be distorted or anachronistic and we can only really rely upon contemporary illustrations, which may in themselves have elements of artistic dependence, and on the actual arms and armour.†

The advent of the complete equipment of metal helmet, corslet, greaves and great shield is usually associated in Greece with the hoplite organization, in which the citizen-militia of the city-states fought pitched battles in closely packed ranks, or the phalanx. This military development is itself closely connected with the contemporary social and political conditions, for it was necessary for a sufficient number of citizens to be able to provide much of their military equipment and there was a parallel movement towards democracy.

The new organization of the Roman army, based on property qualifications, which was affected by Servius Tullius in the sixth century BC, also had both a social and political significance.

The army was divided into ranks with differing equipment and this may well have been an attempt on the part of the king both to swell the number of men available for the army and to gain the support of the class of moderately well-to-do farmers, who would now fight in the battle-line along with the nobles. Now tradition held that the Romans had learned both the use of the hoplite shield and the phalanx from the Etruscans while both from the contemporary illustrations of military events and from the surviving equipment, we must believe the Etruscan did fight in this manner.†

It is hard, however, to equate this military organization with what we know of the social conditions of Etruria. It is possible that the authority of kings could enforce such a unity of military discipline but, by the fifth century BC, political power was moving to the nobles, or *principes*, in the Etruscan city-states. It has, therefore, been suggested that perhaps the great families, or *gentes*, fought as units, much in the manner of the Fabian clan at Cremera, or that the *principes* were able to enlist their clients and other dependants. We hear of attempts to hire

86 The *Aristonothos* krater *with a scene of a sea battle. In the Capitoline Museums, Rome*

87 *Coin of Populonia with hammer and tongs, symbolizing the city's interest in metalworking*

Gaulish mercenaries, yet we cannot explain just how the Etruscan city-states managed to fight battles with well-armed infantrymen, deploying in a disciplined phalanx, generally a socially equalizing form, when at the same time they maintained their aristocratic society. It may be that as the political power passed to the nobles a military crisis arose in Etruria, which might in part explain the decline in strength suffered during the fifth century BC. However, the Etruscans still had a reputation for valour amongst the Romans into the fourth century.†

In naval affairs, again we know more of the outcome of Etruscan activities than of the methods they used. There are few contemporary illustrations of naval actions but these show that, even by the seventh century BC, Etruscan warships had a type of ram and, like the Greeks, their ships were manned by marines, armed as infantrymen, who are shown standing on a high platform stretching from bow to stern. It has been suggested that the painting on the Aristonothos *krater*, of about the middle of the seventh century BC, shows an engagement between a Greek and an Etruscan ship. The former has a long ram and is being rowed into action, whilst the latter has a high hull and ram, no oarsmen are shown and a mast is rigged, at the top of which is perched a spearman (*86*).

Among the rather rare illustrations of other types of Etruscan ship is that of the fine merchantman from the recently discovered Tomb of the Ship at Tarquinia. This ship has a high prow and stern, a lattice running along the bulwarks and two masts, from which square sails hang on spars, which are controlled by a complicated rigging. Attention may also be drawn to the delightful little skiffs, with an eye painted in gay colours upon the bow, to be seen in the paintings of the Tomb of Hunting and Fishing (*107*).

Etruscan prowess at sea was widely accepted in antiquity. Pisaeus, son of Tyrrenus, was credited with the invention of *rostra*, the beaks or rams of warships, and the seas on either side of the Italian peninsula owed their names to the Etruscans, the Adriatic taking its name from Adria, the port near the mouth of the Po, while the Tyrrhenian Sea still bears a Greek form of the Etruscan name. It was also recorded by the ancient authors that the Etruscans had terrorized Greek sailors, who ventured into the Tyrrhenian Sea during the eighth century BC, that their piracy compelled the Greeks of Lipari to adopt a strictly communistic regime, that they colonized Corsica, sailed in the west Mediterranean and even that they contended with the Carthaginians for the possession of an Atlantic island. We also know that a general from Tarquinia took an army to Sicily, that Etruscans sent ships to help the Athenians at Syracuse in 413 BC and, in 307 BC, we hear of eighteen Etruscan ships arriving in Sicily to aid Agothocles in his struggle against the Carthaginians. However, a century later, in 205 BC, the Etruscan cities did not offer ships for Scipio's levy, though they sent wood for ship building and flax for sails.†

TRADE

Such sea power, allied to her vast mineral resources, the wood from her forests and her agricultural potential, provided Etruria with a strong trading position. It is easiest to look at Etruscan trade in two parts: firstly, her sea trade, which brought her into contact with the Greeks, Carthaginians and their predecessors the Phoenicians, together with the other peoples of the east Mediterranean and, secondly, the trade between Etruria and her Italic neighbours and the peoples beyond the Alps. Broadly speaking, and with the exception of the barbarian peoples of the west Mediterranean, in her sea trade, Etruria played the part of a primary producer, exporting her mineral resources in return for great quantities of manufactured goods, while in her dealings with her Italic and northern neighbours, she reversed these rôles, exporting her own finished products.

We have seen that the Greeks told many stories of Etruscan piracy but seamen, especially successful seamen of rival states, have often been called by this name, from the time of Ulysses to the present day. Nevertheless, it is well to bear in mind that goods may travel in other ways than by trade; they may be taken as loot or be dedications and this is particularly likely in the case of goods found at the great sanctuaries of Greece. We know that both Cerveteri (Caere) and Spina had treasuries at Delphi, and we also hear of an Etruscan king who dedicated a throne at Olympia and was said to have been the first non-Greek to make an offering there.† It is possible that the Villanovan and early Etruscan objects, dating from the eighth and seventh centuries BC, which have been found in Greece, may best be explained in these ways and that the vast majority of the imports found in Etruria would have been exchanged for iron, copper and other metallic ores.

Though raw materials remained the principal basis of Etruria's purchasing power in the following centuries, some Etruscan manufactured goods were traded in the Mediterranean area from the sixth century BC onwards. We have seen that Etruscan products, notably gold and bronzework, were of a very high standard and much admired in Greece and trade has been confirmed by the discovery of Etruscan bronzes both in Magna Graecia and Greece, notably the fragment of a tripod stand, probably made at Vulci, which was found at Athens. It is even possible that trade, as well as later collections, played a part in distributing the Etruscan statuettes, presumably of bronze, which were widely scattered.† The distribution of *bucchero*, the pottery type in which the Etruscans excelled, also shows widespread trade; *bucchero* pots, especially *kantharoi*, have been found in the south of France, Spain, at Carthage and other Punic sites including those of Sardinia, the Greek cities of Magna Graecia, in Greece, and as far east as Rhodes and Asia Minor.

Within Italy, the historical contacts between Campania and the Etruscans have already been traced and something of the complicated relationship in the field of the arts; a similar trading relationship existed and southern Lazio, lying in between, benefited from both directions. To the east, the Umbrians and Picenes received many Etruscan manufactured goods in the Orientalizing style and during later periods but a number of Hellenic goods also reached them from the Adriatic, at least by the sixth century BC. To the north, trade continued to cross the Apennine passes into the lower Po Valley, as it had done since the Bronze Age. This penetration was already quite strong in the seventh century BC and its influence, together with Italic goods, even crossed the Alps, there to affect the native styles.

In the sixth century BC, Etruscan objects may have joined with the Greek trade, which entered France from the south coast, after the foundation of Marseille about 600 BC. This trade would have deteriorated with the growing antagonism between the Etruscans and the Phocaean Greeks and it seems that the east Alpine passes, accessible both to the Etruscan colonies now established in the Po Valley and to the Greek trade in the Adriatic, were chiefly used. The list of Etruscan bronzes, dating from the sixth century onwards, found north of the Alps is extensive and includes the *oinochoe* (*61*) which was probably made at Vulci but which was found near Trier in south-west Germany. Like so many other Etruscan exports to the north, this formed part of a wine service, equipment much sought after by the Gaulish chieftains, so that the Etruscan type of 'beaked flagon' influenced the designs of the *La Tène* bronzesmiths.

For long, the Etruscans conducted their trade without the use of coinage. Many of the Greek cities of the west had begun to strike coins by the middle of the sixth century and the earliest known coins from Etruria are of Phocaean type, dating towards the end of that century. About 500 BC, some of the Etruscan cities began to mint and followed the Greek practice in using silver and, in times of crisis, gold, though their coinage was principally of bronze. Etruscan coins are seldom distinguished in design; one side was often left flat, without a type, while upon the other a gorgon, chimera or griffin frequently appears, though the cities sometimes indicated their name or chose a more individual emblem, like the hammer and tongs on the coins of Populonia (*87*). A standard weight appears to have been based upon the Euboic-Attic system, in turn linked with the Sicilian *litra*, and many of the coins bear numerals of the decimal system, xxv, x and v, indicating their relative value. The Etruscan cities continued to mint through the Classical and into the Hellenistic period before becoming absorbed into the Roman monetary system.

There must also have been considerable traffic between the cities and towns of Etruria and this brings us to a consideration of the roads and means of transport. In the third and second centuries BC, the great, paved, Roman military highways were built across Etruria, their routes fanning out from Rome. The line of the *via Aurelia* follows the coast to Pisa and that of the *via Clodia*, passing to the west of Lake Bracciano, leads on to Blera and Saturnia. The route of the *via Cassia*, skirting the lakes of Vico and Bolsena, continues to Chiusi, Arezzo and on to Florence, while that of the *via Amerina* runs through S Maria di Falleri (Falerii Novi) and on to the middle Tiber Valley. The *via Flaminia* crosses the territory of the Faliscans, before continuing to the Adriatic coast.

All these roads led to Rome and served her military needs, while uniting the whole region with the capital but they often disregarded the local requirements of communities which had grown up within an older framework. Sometimes, however, the Roman roads followed existing routes, for the Etruscans had been road builders long before their conquest. A wider understanding of their road system has recently been gained from a careful survey of southern Etruria, chiefly in the areas around Veii. A good example of a road serving specifically Etruscan needs is that which runs from Pyrgi and Cerveteri (Caere) eastwards to Veii, whence another road led on to Palestrina (Praeneste), thus ignoring Rome. It is also interesting to note the commanding position held by Veii within her own territory; this is emphasized by the number of roads radiating from her gates.

88 A lady riding in a cart on her journey to the underworld, shown in a relief on a sarcophagus from Vulci. In the Museum of Fine Arts, Boston

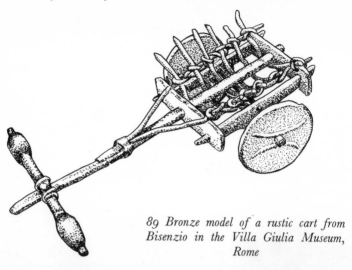

89 Bronze model of a rustic cart from Bisenzio in the Villa Giulia Museum, Rome

Paved road surfaces or cobbles are only known in urban areas or their immediate vicinity but the Etruscan road builders were often most adventurous in their methods. They frequently cut a highway through the living rock, placing a drainage ditch at the side, and, on occasions, they diverted the waters of a stream to utilize its bed or made use of the rock as a bridgeway. We know, too, of stone foundations built to support the wooden beams of bridges and, in Hellenistic times, bridges were built with true arches in stone.

Horses, mules and donkeys were used to ride or as beasts of burden; there are numerous illustrations of boys and men riding and the loaded pack mules, to be seen on a sarcophagus in Perugia, have already been mentioned (*85*). Oxen are shown, yoked to ploughs, and wheeled vehicles, drawn by horses or mules, are also well documented. The metal fittings from chariots are known from several tombs of the seventh century BC and the Monteleone chariot has been described (*34*). Such a magnificent work of art was clearly intended for cere-monial occasions but chariots were also used for racing and, in the later bas-reliefs, may often be seen carrying distinguished men on their journey to the underworld. Four-wheeled vehicles were known by the seventh century but a two-wheeled type of cart is most often shown in the representations. It is the *carpentum*, the type of cart in which Lucius Tarquinius and Tanaquil travelled to Rome (p. 27), whose history there has been traced by Heurgon, showing that it was often used by women. In Etruria, these two-wheeled carts are to be seen, frequently with women on their journey to the underworld (*88*). Sometimes the carts are very elegant, with hooped covers decorated with fringes, and shown with their occupants reclining inside (*96*). Other examples are more rustic, like the bronze model from Bisenzio, which clearly copies a cart built of rough boarding with lashed cross-pieces and with the yoke bound to the pole with what looks like a leather thong (*89*), or the type seen on the *stelai* from Bologna, whose frames appear to be made of wickerwork (*84*).

INDUSTRY AND AGRICULTURE

In the days of their prosperity, the economy of the Etruscans was soundly based upon both industry and agriculture. The wide variety of goods produced in the region includes the fine pottery from several schools, as well as local wares; the gold and bronzework, so widely exported, and objects of iron; vehicles, furniture and smaller wooden things; the leather goods, from harness and armour to bags and shoes, famous in antiquity, and the cloth, often richly dyed.

As yet we know little of the workshops which produced these goods, though there were kilns and metalworking areas at Marzabotto, together with evidence of local weaving. The metal of some craft tools, like axe blades, hammers, chisels, adzes, saws and others has survived, and, occasionally, we may see how they were hafted from representations, usually showing some mythical craftsman, like Icarus (*91*). To the activities of the potters, smiths, carpenters, leatherworkers, weavers and dyers, we may add that of the miners, masons, timber-men working in the forests, the charcoal burners and agricultural workers.

By far the most important industrial process, however, was the exploitation of the vast mineral resources of copper, tin, lead, silver and, above all, of iron, which lay in the region. The main mining area was within the territory of Populonia, on Elba, in the Colline Metallifere and around Campiglia Marittima, some twenty kilometres (twelve miles) to the north-east

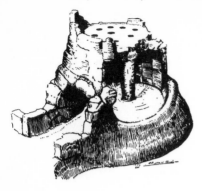

90 Diagrammatic drawing of a smelting furnace, which was found in the Val Fucinaia in the territory of Populonia

of the city. Here, and particularly in the area of Val Fucinaia, the mining activity appears to date back to at least the eighth century BC. There is evidence of opencast mining, shafts and galleries, which follow the seams of ore and smelting furnaces have been found, mainly used for the copper ores. These furnaces were built in the form of a truncated cone, less than two metres (seven feet) in diameter at the base, and were lined with refractory tiles; a perforated partition divided the upper from the lower chamber, which was provided with a small door. Ore and charcoal were placed in the upper chamber and a fire lit below; the iron oxide separated out and remained in the upper chamber, while the molten copper flowed through the perforations into the lower chamber, where it could be collected (*90*).

The greatest source of iron was on the island of Elba and it is probable that, at first, the smelting took place there, though local fuel supplies must soon have become exhausted. The early tombs at Populonia became covered by an enormous quantity of slag which was the industrial residue from the smelting of local ores in this area, a process which must have begun by the fourth century BC and continued for three centuries or more. The volume has been estimated at two million tons, itself now a source of ore, which can be extracted by the more efficient modern methods. At this time the ore of Elba was smelted locally and then shipped to exchange stations, where it was either resold or, as at a port near Naples, the modern Pozzuoli, it was manufactured into weapons and tools.†

Before Scipio set sail in 205 BC for Africa and the campaign which was to end the Second Punic War, he called for a levy of expeditionary supplies; Etruria gave generously and Livy gives a list of contributions promised by the cities. Populonia sent iron and Tarquinia linen for sail-cloth, while Cerveteri (Caere) gave grain and other goods. Volterra (Volaterrae) supplied material for shipbuilding, probably the hardwood needed for keels and frames, as well as grain; Arezzo (Arretium) emerged as an industrial power, providing three thousand helmets and shields, fifty thousand spears of various kinds, together with enough axes, spades, sickles, baskets and hand-mills to equip forty ships. Roselle (Rusellae), Chiusi (Clusium), and Perugia (Perusia) gave grain and pine for shipbuilding. In this list both the relative decline of the coastal areas to the wealth of the northern cities is evident, as well as the balance of the mineral and agricultural resources of Etruria, together with those of the forests.†

Etruria was once well-wooded and even in southern Etruria as late as the end of the fourth century BC, the forests were formidable enough to inspire fear in the hearts of Roman soldiers (p. 36). The beech trees from central Italy were capable of providing the keel of an Etruscan ship in a single piece, and the long, straight timber for beams; we have seen how much wood was used for architecture in Etruria. Wood was, of course, used for a multitude of other things from vehicles and ploughs to weapons and tools, from furniture to cosmetic boxes and many varieties of tree were employed. Analysis has shown that oak, elm, beech, pine, maple, willow, viburnum and box-wood were used, as well as imported ebony and cork, used for sealing vases and some statues were carved from vine. Wood was also extensively used as fuel for the industrial furnaces and, as charcoal, for cooking and heating the houses. We do not know the extent nor the pace of the progressive deforestation of Etruria but we may be sure it has affected the climate of the region, making it hotter and drier.†

Perhaps the Etruscans already realized the potential danger of the deforestation of the hillsides, causing soil erosion and creating swamps in the valleys and coastal plain, which in turn would encourage the spread of deadly malaria. At any rate, they were extraordinarily skilled and careful in handling the water resources of their land. They probably cut a canal near Adria and knew how to tap underground water supplies and drain

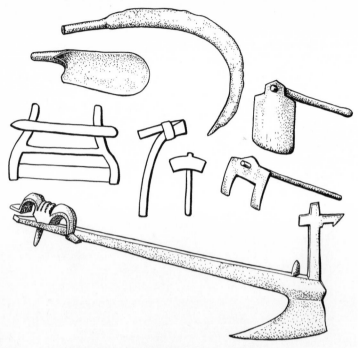

91 Some types of woodworking and agricultural tools

swamps and lakes. Evidence for such skills comes from the tuff region of southern Etruria, where a widespread system of *cuniculi* is known. These subterranean passages, cut through the rock and linked to the fresh air by shafts with steps like ladders hewn into the sides, carried water from one valley to another. This was an effective way both of controlling the water supply and of preventing soil erosion. It also proved extremely effective in stopping the soft rock being channelled into deep gullies, a result clearly shown in air-photographs.†

Etruria was also famed in antiquity for its agricultural wealth: indeed the prodigal fertility of the soil was put forward as cause for Etruscan decadence. The soil was rich and the rainfall moderate, both in winter and summer; the good yield of the harvests was noted and the quality of the grain. This was particularly true of the region of the upper Tiber and its tributaries, a district which was probably already supplying corn to

Rome in the fifth century BC. We know little of the actual methods of farming, since the Etruscans did not often illustrate the working lives of the poor, although in 310 BC the Consul's brother armed himself with sickles and two hunting spears in order to pass unnoticed in Etruria. A votive group of model tools from Talamone adds to our knowledge; among them are a chopper, sickle, hoes and ploughs (*91*) and to these we may add shears, pruning knives, hand-mills and grain measures, all occasionally seen in the museums. The model plough from Talamone has a guiding handle and a straight blade, which would not have turned the clod. A similar plough may be seen in a fourth-century model from Arezzo, showing a ploughman with yoked oxen (*92*).†

Of other important crops, flax was grown for linen and the olive (perhaps a late-comer to Etruria, as the Etruscan word for 'oil' is derived from Greek) produced both cooking fat and fuel. There are rare scenes of the grape harvest, when the grapes were gathered into large baskets; the wines of Etruria were known in Greece by the Hellenistic period, though they were

92 Model of a ploughman with yoked oxen from Arezzo in the Villa Giulia Museum, Rome

*93 Kitchen scenes from the Golini Tomb, Orvieto; paintings now in Florence
Archaeological Museum*

never, perhaps, considered very outstanding by the Romans.
For evidence of other fruits, vegetables and flowers, we have to
rely mainly upon representations in floral designs, some of
which may be artistic borrowings. However, we may see the
vine, pomegranate, apples and blackberries, as well as the
artichoke, pea and bean and note convolvulus, crocus, poppy,
lily, acanthus, laurel and palm in decorative motifs. Some
plants were considered to be of good or evil omen.†

The Etruscans reared chickens, ducks, geese and guinea fowl
and their eggs are sometimes found in tombs. They bred pigs
and Polybius gives a vivid description of swineherds, not driving
their charges from behind as was usual in Greece, but leading
them, occasionally blowing a note upon a trumpet, which the
pigs recognized. The Etruscans stocked goats, cattle and sheep;
some regional cheese later became famous and bronze graters,
possibly used for cheese, may sometimes be seen in museums.†

Wool was woven into cloth and either bleached or dyed with
many different colours. Hunting provided the meat of wild
pig, deer, hares, doves and waterfowl and we also hear of the
fresh-water lakes being stocked with fish. The sea must have
supplied much the same variety of fish as it does today, including tunny, as Strabo saw a watch-station on the coast, and
tortoise eggs were still available until very recent times. Some
local recipes may well have been enjoyed by the Etruscans of
old; fish stuffed with rosemary, or roast pork similarly flavoured
or pork liver cooked with bay leaves. We may feel sure that
such herbs were used to flavour the food, as honey was to sweeten
it and salt to preserve it.†

Spits and grills were used for cooking, as well as saucepans
for boiling liquids and ovens for baking. One of the very rare
working scenes from Etruria is actually of a kitchen; the paintings were originally in the Golini Tomb near Orvieto, dating
to the fourth century BC, but now have been moved to the
Archaeological Museum at Florence (*93*). One scene shows meat
hanging ready in the open air; there is a carcass of beef, venison,
a hare and a brace of birds. One cook is about to hold a frying-
pan over the flames of an oven and another is ready with a
saucepan, while a storage *pithos* stands nearby. On another wall,
the painting shows a cook chopping meat which he will cook
over a small open fire, while a second is preparing food by
pounding it with two pestles, one held in either hand, over a
large mortar. Beside him is a flute player, a figure seen so often
in Etruscan illustrations, while an elegant woman supervises
a slave, who is about to lift one of the four tables, already laden
with food for the banquet, including bread, a pomegranate and
bunches of black grapes.

An atmosphere of orderliness pervades what we know of the
Etruscans' management of the land in which they lived. We
need have little doubt that they were excellent agriculturalists
but there is a feeling, too, of responsibility beyond material
things. Boundaries were sacred, plants of good or bad omen,
while celestial and terrestrial prodigies were carefully examined;
this religious core of Etruscan life will be described in the
following chapter.

8

Religion, government and
social structure

Religion was always closely interwoven with the secular life of
the Etruscans. Yet, while we know comparatively little about
the political organization of the city-states, we have several
sources of information to help us understand Etruscan religion.
Though there are both Etruscan texts and scenes illustrating
religious forms, the imbalance of our evidence chiefly rests upon
the far greater interest taken by the Romans in those aspects
of Etruscan life which had most deeply affected their own
traditions. Among these were some of their ceremonial customs
and religious attitudes, especially concerning the art of divination.

RELIGION

The Etruscans won a reputation for themselves in antiquity as
being a uniquely religious people.† We know something of the
Etruscans' conception of the gods and man's place in the world
and of the difference between their religious attitudes and that
of their contemporaries, the Greeks, and their neighbours, the
Romans.

The Greeks did feel the force of all-powerful fate and were
drawn to consult the oracles of the gods and other forms of
divination. But they were also capable of seeing man as the
measure of all things and of exalting human reason, while the
Romans built up a legalistic conception of the relationship
between the gods and men. These attitudes seem quite alien
to the Etruscans; among them there existed a profound, almost
fatalistic, belief in destiny and the immutable course of divine
will, in which the span of nations and men was preordained

and a deep conviction that man's highest duty was to seek to understand and live within these prescribed laws.

Rules of conduct, often expressed in ritual observations, had to be minutely fulfilled and, since the Etruscans believed that the will of the gods was shown by portents in the material world, it was man's obligation to observe such signs and to interpret them correctly. The Etruscans' attitude to portents was summed up by Seneca: 'Whereas we (the Romans) believe lightning to be released as a result of the collision of the clouds, they (the Etruscans) believe that clouds collide so as to release lightning, for as they attribute all to the deity, they are led to believe not that things have a meaning in so far as they occur, but rather that they occur because they must have a meaning'.† Indeed, much of the Etruscans' best intellectual effort was devoted to this anxious questioning and interpretation of destiny. The Etruscans were renowned in antiquity both for their scrupulous attention to correct ritual formulae and for their skill in the art of divination, by which they could regulate their present and future actions.

To help them in these aims, the Etruscans believed they had knowledge revealed from supernatural sources. It was said that once a ploughman at Tarquinia saw a figure spring from the furrow, who had the appearance of a boy but the wisdom of a seer. This strange boy was called Tages; a crowd gathered round him and he expounded the art of divination. This was written down and as new facts became known they were added to the fund of knowledge.† Again, it was said that a nymph, Vegoia, had revealed to Arruns Velthumnus of Clusium (modern Chiusi) information concerning the beginning of the world and the unchanging laws of boundaries. This, too, was committed to writing and, in the first century BC, a Latin translation was made, fragments of which have come down to us.

Thus revealed sources and added experience were included in the Etruscan sacred books on ritual and divination. Etruscan priests were learned in this traditional doctrine, the *Etrusca Disciplina*, as the Romans called it, and were guided by it in their search for signs from the gods and their interpretation of such prodigies. We have a number of accounts of the replies given by Etruscan haruspices, when they were consulted by the

Roman state about various alarming omens; one tells of strange noises, heard in 56 BC in the neighbourhood of Rome. The state consulted the haruspices who named the gods who should be propitiated and gave the causes of their anger, which included the disregard of ritual, profanation of sacred places, the breaking of oaths, and the murder of ambassadors. Finally, they told the meaning of the portent, that care should be taken that no danger should come to the state through discord between the nobles.†

Apart from the interpretation of prodigies, the Etruscan priests sought to discover the will of the gods by various forms of divination, chiefly the observation of thunder and lightning, the examination of the entrails, and especially the liver as the seat of life, of sacrificed animals and the flight of birds. The principle followed in the former method was to divide the dome of the sky into sixteen parts, radiating from the observer, who faced south. The eight regions to the left, to the east, were favourable and those to the west were adverse. The region of the sky where lightning appeared was observed and the lightning was divided further into types, the direction in which it travelled and the point of impact. Lightning could be sent by nine gods but there were eleven types in all, since Jupiter could hurl three sorts of thunderbolt. By observing all these characteristics, the meaning of the lightning might be interpreted. The Etruscans believed that the fortunes of both men and cities could thus be foretold and that lightning might even be summoned by means of prayer and ritual.†

Sixteen gods were allotted the regions of the sky. These names correspond mainly, though not precisely, with those written on the sixteen outer compartments of the bronze model of a sheep's liver found at Piacenza, which must have been a device to aid divination by haruspicy (94). This shows that the liver, used in divination, was considered as a microcosm of the universe, divided as was the sky, a concept expressed in Latin by the word '*templum*'. In all, there are forty spaces on the Piacenza liver and among the names written on them are some identified as groups, or colleges, of gods, of which we also hear in the Roman sources. These were the nameless *Dii Superiores* or *Involuti*, equivalent, it seems, to the fates, whom even Jupiter could not oppose and who were consulted by him on hurling his

94 Bronze model of a sheep's liver from Piacenza

third and final thunderbolt. Secondly there were the *Dii Consentes* or *Complices*, a council of twelve gods, which Jupiter consulted before throwing his second thunderbolt.†

Some gods were, therefore, anonymous and shrouded in mystery; in the Roman sources, other gods are called by their Latin or Italic names, many also identifiable with the gods of Greece. We may give some gods their Etruscan names, mainly deduced from the inscriptions written on offerings and on the mirrors, whose engraved scenes provide a wealth of information. These scenes often show recognizable gods with their Etruscan names written beside them. They also demonstrate how familiar the Etruscans were with Greek mythology, sometimes depicting variants on the accepted stories and sometimes misunderstanding them. Occasionally, too, Etruscan legends are presented, like the story of Tages or that of Cacus, shown as a seer, who may be involved in a contest with the Vibenna brothers. In the scene engraved on the mirror illustrated here, a winged figure, whose name, *Chalchas*, is written beside him, is shown in the act of divining *(95)*.

Of the major gods, Jupiter was called Tin or Tinia by the Etruscans and his consort, Juno, was called Uni; she was the supreme deity of Veii, where her priesthood was hereditary. These two gods were grouped with Minerva, Etruscan Menrva, in the Capitoline triad. Neptune was called Nethuns and was

95 Bronze mirror with an engraved scene of Chalchas *examining the liver of a sacrificed animal. In the Vatican Museum, Rome*

the great god of Vetulonia; Mars was named Maris and Venus was called Turan, a name which may go back to the word *turannos*, known in western Asia Minor, and which may signify 'lady' or 'mistress' in this context. Vulcan was called Sethlans and was worshipped in Perugia; Mercury was Turms, who appears as a guide for departing souls. Bacchus has the strange name of Fufluns, probably an Etruscan corruption of a Greek form of the god's name 'Byblinos'. Some Greek names were hardly altered; Apollo appears as Apulu or Aplu and his sister, Artemis, as Artumes or Aritimi, while the Greek hero Herakles became Hercle in Etruscan and, in Latin, Hercules. We know,

too, the names of some local divinities. Greek sources mention
the names of Leucothea or Eileithyia for the goddess, who was
worshipped at Pyrgi; there was a cult of Nortia at Bolsena
(Volsinii), where a nail was struck into the wall of the temple
each year, to denote the passing of time and it was at the shrine
of Voltumna, whom Varro called the chief god of Etruria, that
people from the twelve cities assembled every year.†

A certain amount is known of the priesthood and, in late
centuries, the maintenance of the *Etrusca Disciplina*. Priests
were drawn from the noble class and we know some details
of the careers of these men from funerary inscriptions and may
see the effigy of a haruspex on a cinerary chest at Volterra (*96*).
The priestly dress included a fringed mantle, fastened with a
fibula, and a high, conical hat (*97*) and priests are sometimes
shown holding a curved stick, the *lituus* of the Roman augur.
The haruspices must generally have had a formidable reputation but this had fallen into some disrepute at Rome by the
second century BC, when Cato remarked that he could not
understand how one 'soothsayer doesn't laugh when he sees

*96 Cinerary chest with an effigy of a
haruspex in Volterra Archaeological
Museum*

*97 Bronze statuette of an
Etruscan priest in the Vatican
Museum, Rome*

157

another soothsayer'. Yet, probably by the second century BC, the Roman senate took action to preserve the Etruscan discipline, and in the first century BC we hear of members of great Etruscan families, like the Caecinae or the Tarquitii, translating Etruscan texts into Latin and handing their knowledge from father to son. Eminent Romans had Etruscan haruspices in their personal entourage, like Spurinna, who warned Julius Caesar of the Ides of March, and, by the first century AD, a college of sixty haruspices had been set up. Gatherings were still taking place at the shrine of Voltumna in the reign of Constantine, early in the fourth century AD. As late as AD 410, when the oracles of Greece were silent and the Empire had been Christian for a hundred years, Etruscan haruspices offered to summon lightning to repel Alaric from the walls of Rome.†

We have little information about rites performed in the temples and only occasional scenes of sacrificial animals led to an altar on which a flame is burning, very similar to Greek and Roman illustrations. We know such sacrifices could be offered as propitiations to the gods, to invoke their aid or to seek their will, by the rules of divination. The Etruscans were much given to offering sacrifices, and it is likely that an exact calendar for such services existed, as well as the ritual formulae used at the dedication of altars and temples and the founding of cities.†

We also have some glimpses in the representational scenes of the forms followed at marriages and funerals; a relief in Chiusi shows a couple sitting, facing one another, while a covering is held over their heads, the symbol of the marriage bond, and a priest and a flute player stand nearby (*98*). Some

98 Bas-relief of a wedding scene in Chiusi Archaeological Museum

99 Bas-relief of a funerary scene on a cippus *from Chiusi. In the British Museum*

processions are also shown and there are a number of scenes showing funerary customs; we may see the corpse laid on a high couch, surrounded by mourners, and imagine a lying-in-state, before the procession to the tomb (*99*).

The funerary games are often illustrated. Some were athletic sports and others would seem appropriate at a fair, but very occasionally a more bloodthirsty rite appears. In the Tomb of

100 Scene of funerary games and rites from the Tomb of the Augurs, Tarquinia

the Augurs at Tarquinia, dated towards the end of the sixth century BC, and next to an ordinary wrestling match, there is shown a man, blindfolded and with a club in his hand, who is viciously attacked by a dog, held on a leash by a masked man, whose name, *Phersu*, is written beside him (*100*). This word is found in Latin as *persona*, meaning a mask, an actor or the part he played, and thence has passed into several European languages. This scene has been interpreted in differing ways. Some see in it the enactment of a myth concerning Hercules, others believe it may show a recollection of ancient rites with human sacrifice. Perhaps, too, the Etruscans carried rituals of this type with them into Campania. The Oscan peoples practised gladiatorial combats and these came from Campania to Rome, where they were first held in 264 BC, at the funerary games of the consul's father.†

It is equally difficult to describe or rationalize Etruscan beliefs concerning the afterlife. Even in Villanovan times, when the dead were cremated, their ashes were sometimes placed in model huts, implying some belief in the comforting continuation of earthly forms after death. Also, the Canopic urns from Chiusi, with their lids modelled as human heads, which were sometimes set upon a chair in front of a table, would seem to suggest a conception that even the cremated dead required permanent and familiar surroundings, although the form of funerary rite might be taken to imply a release from earthly bonds. The tombs, which reproduce the interior of a house and its contents, evoke a similar idea that the spirit of the dead, in some sense, was believed to live on in the tomb, though this need not exclude a conception of the soul's journey into a world beyond the tomb. The painted scenes in the earlier tombs show little but joy, but from the fourth century BC onwards, there accumulates a feeling of the dread of death. The figure of *Charun* appears; the name is borrowed from that of the ferryman whom the Greeks believed carried the souls across the River Styx, and it is possible that there were also Greek prototypes for demons in the underworld, since we know Polygnotos showed them there in his famous painting at Delphi.†

In Etruria the presence of *Charun* becomes familiar in scenes illustrating the departure of the dead. He is shown as a grotesque figure with a hideous face, often painted green/blue, with wings and holding a mallet in his hand. Winged female figures frequently accompany him; they were called *Vanths* and hold torches or serpents. In the paintings from the Golini Tomb, we see a scene set in the underworld with a banquet spread before Hades (or Pluto; Latin Orcus) and Persephone (Latin Proserpina). At Tarquinia in the later chamber of the Tomb of Orcus these rulers of the underworld again appear and with them figures from Homeric epic, including Teiresias, and Theseus, shown as a young man, menaced by a ghastly demon, *Tuchulcha*, holding snakes in his hands. These representations may simply be taken as poetic imagery of the underworld and certainly should not be taken too literally as an Etruscan conception of life after death; rather, we should note that many of the departing souls, of the *Vanths* who accompany them, hold scrolls in their hands and it may be that some idea of judgment had developed, as had a belief in the saving power of ritual.

GOVERNMENT

We have seen how closely religious forms were interwoven with secular life in Etruria, so that portents, directly ascribed to the gods, could be interpreted in a highly political manner. There can be little doubt that this characteristic coloured much of the administration of the city-states of Etruria and it may also be observed in their corporate assembly.

Every year, it seems, people from the twelve cities of Etruria met at the shrine of Voltumna, the *Fanum Voltumnae*, which we know was situated within the territory of Volsinii (modern Bolsena), and at least on some occasions, representatives of the city-states there discussed military and political affairs.† It is also likely that the Etruscan states had followed the example set by the league of twelve Greek cities in Asia Minor. Nevertheless conditions did not remain unchanging down the centuries; as one or another of the Etruscan cities grew or waned in power, no doubt the political leadership passed from city to city. The bond between the Etruscan states must primarily have been religious and it may be suggested that, just as the Greeks gathered at Delphi or Olympia to hold pan-Hellenic festivals, so the Etruscans assembled at the *Fanum Voltumnae* for games and a great fair, at which, in times of crisis, delegates from the city-states could exchange opinion and accept or reject plans for common action. Officials were elected at these meetings. In early times, perhaps, kings were chosen and later, priests, but we do not know their duties or how the federation was organized.

Though we do not hear of such bitter strife as was waged among the Greek city-states, it is clear that the system of the Etruscan states had also grown to a mature and definitive form at a time when the cities and peoples were still living in comparative isolation one from another. Thus later generations inherited a political system in which the Etruscan cities found it hard to unite in common action. This fact is demonstrated throughout their independent history; they fought many of their wars alone, or with changing alliances, and they had individual truces or treaties with Rome. So we may conclude that they formed a loose confederation of autonomous city-states, linked by their religious ties, their common language and, on some occasions, by their mutual interests.

At a time when the political organization of the Italic peoples was still predominantly tribal, we always hear of the administration of Etruria based upon the city-states, resembling those of Greece or Magna Graecia, and that these cities gave their names to the peoples, just as the Athenians took their name from Athens. Though our sources mention the twelve cities of Etruria,† no ancient list has come down to us and there has been some modern speculation as to which cities were included. There is no need to believe that the list remained unaltered down the centuries; indeed we know the number was changed in Imperial times. A modern suggestion lists Caere (modern Cerveteri), Tarquinii (modern Tarquinia), Vulci, Rusellae (modern Roselle), Vetulonia, Volsinii (modern Bolsena), Clusium (modern Chiusi), Perusia (modern Perugia), Cortona, Arretium (modern Arezzo) and Volaterrae (modern Volterra), with Populonia taking the place of Veii at her fall.

The relationship between these states and the Etruscan colonies in Campania and the Po Valley is also speculative, as is that between the cities and the larger towns within their territories, like, for example, Norchia, Talamone, Pisa or Fiesole (Faesulae). Though there is some evidence that the smaller towns suffered as the cities grew in strength, later inscriptions, dating mainly from after the conquest, suggest at least some degree of local organization.

Neither the ancient sources nor the epigraphic evidence allow us to do more than sketch the outline of the political development within the Etruscan states. In early times there were monarchies, the institution probably emerging as the states took form. The king was called *lauchme*, or *lauchume* in Etruscan. On analogy with other states, the kings probably held the religious, military and judicial authority. The Etruscans seemed to have called upon their king, probably in the latter capacity, on the ninth day, which implies that they, like the Romans, worked for eight days and held a market on the ninth. Concerning the Etruscan manner of reckoning time, their century has been described (p. 17) and the ceremony of hammering a nail into the wall of the temple of Nortia to mark the passing of a year, a symbolic act shown on some of the scenes engraved on mirrors. We know the Etruscan word for year, *avil*, from many funerary inscriptions. The lunar months began with the new moon; several names of the months are known; the full moon was marked by the Ides and the ninth day was counted back from this point, like the Roman *nones*. Unlike the Romans, however, the Etruscans reckoned each day from noon to high noon.

Roman tradition has preserved some vivid details of the regal insignia of Etruscan kings, as it was believed that these had been accepted by the kings of Rome and then survived among the symbols of office of the Roman magistrates and, we might add, of later local Etruscan magistrates. They were also perpetuated in the ceremonies surrounding a victorious general, as he celebrated his triumph in a great procession through the streets of Rome.

Livy records that he personally believed that Romulus had followed Etruscan custom in assuming the regal dignity of twelve attendants, or lictors, and added that the curule stool and *toga praetexta*, both among the insignia of Roman magistrates, also came from Etruria. With the advent of the Republic, the lictors carried the *fasces*, the bundles of rods with an axe at the centre, before the consuls and a tradition, which may go back to Cato's *Origines*, mentions that these symbols of authority were attributed to the Etruscans and even specifies their origin at Vetulonia.

Dionysius of Halicarnassus recounts how, after Lucius Tarquinius the Elder of Rome had defeated the Etruscans in battle,
they brought him their emblems of royalty, which, he says, were
'a crown of gold, an ivory throne, a sceptre with an eagle
perched on its head, a purple tunic decorated with gold and an
embroidered purple robe', which was semicircular in shape.
There is little need to doubt the spirit of these traditions, though
they may err in detail, since late Republican authors were apt
to believe that Roman ceremonial had not altered from the time
of the Tarquins down to their own day. Nevertheless, the
archaeological evidence amply supports the traditions, demon-
strating that the Etruscans did use many of the insignia attributed to them, though not all in the same century.†

A small iron model of a *fascis* has been found in the seventh-
century Tomb of the Lictor at Vetulonia (*101*); this has a
double-bladed axe, like that brandished by *Avele Feluske* on his
stele (*81*), though only single-bladed axes are known on representations of Roman *fasces*. A painted plaque from Cerveteri
(Caere), dating towards the end of sixth century BC, shows a
dignitary, perhaps a king, seated upon a folding stool, which
has ivory decorations (*102*); this type was to become the curule

101 Model of a fascis
*from the Tomb of the
Lictor, Vetulonia*

102 A seated dignitary shown on a Campana plaque from Cerveteri. In the Louvre Museum, Paris

103 Vel Saties from the François Tomb, Vulci; painting now in the Torlonia Museum, Rome

stool of Roman magistrates. He wears a short purple cloak and holds a sceptre and, although this example has no symbol at the top, a figure painted on the somewhat earlier Boccanera slabs does carry a rod with an animal at the end. Such insignia of Roman magistrates and generals at their triumph remained remarkably consistent, recalling their ancient origin, but their clothes were more vulnerable to the fashions of the time.

In the third century BC, Etruscans of good family wore long, white cloaks with a border comparable with the *toga praetexta*, white with its purple border, which was worn by Roman magistrates and free-born boys, and whose origin was attributed to the Etruscans in antiquity.† Again, in the François Tomb of Vulci, probably painted in the second or early first century BC, there is shown the figure of Nestor, wearing a long purple cloak, which must represent a contemporary Etruscan idea of royal attire, and *Vel Saties* is seen wrapped in a beautiful purple cloak, which, though it is not semicircular as described by Dionysius, is embroidered with the forms of dancing warriors, surely comparable to the *toga picta*, worn by generals during their triumphal procession through the streets of Rome in late Republican times (*103*).

The primitive monarchies of the Mediterranean world gradually gave way to a broadening of political power; this movement is seen in the Greek cities, at Rome, where tradition states the last king was expelled in 509 BC, and a similar trend occurred amongst the contemporary Punic peoples. Though our evidence is extremely slight, it is probable that the same process took place in Etruria, and we may guess that a part was played by the class of people represented by the neat rows of well-to-do tombs of the time. By the end of the fifth century, to the indignation of other Etruscan states, Veii reverted to a monarchy in a moment of crisis.†

By this time, political power in Etruria had probably generally passed to the order of nobles, or *principes*, formed by members of the great families. This order provided an assembly, analogous to the Roman Senate, which appears to have delegated its authority to magistrates, chosen annually from among their own number. From many funerary inscriptions, dating mainly to the period after the conquest, which describe the careers of distinguished men, we know the names of different magistracies. We hear of *purth*, *zilath* and *maru* and, though it may seem reasonable to suppose that these magistracies formed some sort of college and hierarchy of magistracies, like those of Rome, we do not yet know their precise significance. These magistracies could be held more than once and at a young age; an inscription from Vulci tells of a man who had been *zilath* seven times and *purth* once and who died at the age of seventy-two years. A second funerary inscription, probably that of his son, speaks of a young man who died when he was twenty-five years old, having been *zilath*.† It is representations of such distinguished men that we see on the funerary reliefs of Volterra and other cities; they are shown on their journey to the underworld, riding in chariots, with the bundle of rods and trumpets carried before them and with attendants bearing their stool and writing materials, the symbols of their judicial office.

There is little evidence to help us define the position of the other classes. Though the number of ruling families, or *gentes*, was large, the gulf which divided them from the rest of the community appears always to have remained wide. This division in society may have been crossed by a widespread system of clientage in which a great man gave his protection to a subordinate in return for loyal service. Though this aristocratic society continued in Etruria, we hear of no social upheavals until, at the end of the fourth century BC, the great family of the Cilnii were expelled from Arezzo (Arretium).

Fifty years later, in 265 BC, after the defeat of the Etruscan cities, another social revolution took place, this time at Bolsena (Volsinii) and, though we cannot grasp the details of what occurred, the main outline is clear. It was said that the nobles had abdicated many of their powers, enfranchising some of their slaves and allowing them into the assembly. These immediately took advantage of the situation, instituting a redivision of property, refusing the former nobles permission to attend the assembly or to banquet together and demanding the rights of inter-marriage. The nobles appealed to Rome; they were betrayed and many were murdered in their prison before the Romans arrived and sacked the city, subsequently moving it to a less defensible position.† No story could speak more clearly of the deep division of Etruscan society at this date.

SOCIAL STRUCTURE

As in all strongly aristocratic states, Etruscan society was based upon a firmly knit system of families or *gentes*. Both the groups of funerary inscriptions from family tombs and the individual memorials of the dead provide much evidence for a deep family feeling; few inscriptions are more illustrative than that written on the scroll held by *Lars Pulenas* of Tarquinia (*112*), which records the names of his father, uncle, grandfather and even great-grandfather.

Genealogies stretching over generations have been built up from the inscriptions found together in family tombs and these show that the Etruscans, unlike the Greeks but in common with the Romans, used a personal name followed by a patronymic, or name derived from the father, so that a family name passed from a father to his children. Unlike the Romans, however, the Etruscans frequently placed the names of both their father and mother on their tombs, so that one funerary inscription, for example, reads '*Larth Arnthal Plecus clan Ramthasc Apatrual*' or 'Lars son of Arruns Pleco and Ramtha Apatronia'.†

There can be no doubt that Etruscan ladies were given a place in society which was not enjoyed by those of Greece or Rome in early Republican days. Their status is indicated by the wealth they possessed, from the time of *Larthia*, buried in the Regolini-Galassi Tomb at the middle of the seventh century BC, and on down the generations, as well as the place of honour often reserved for them in the tombs. We may also turn to the few stories we possess of Etruscan women, chiefly told of the wives of the Tarquins by Roman authors, who found it extremely hard to imagine behaviour so different from their own ideas of womanly propriety.

Tanaquil, the high-born Etruscan wife of Lucius Tarquinius the Elder, was learned in interpreting portents, for she foretold the success of her husband (p. 27). She was very much the mistress of the situation when, after the death of her husband, she set aside her own sons in order that her son-in-law, Servius Tullius, might become king of Rome. The stories told of the younger Tarquins and their wives are no more clear in detail and no less amazing. In the account of Tarquinius Superbus' seizure of power, his wife, the headstrong Tullia, not only drives her cart into the Forum and over the body of her dead father but she is the first to proclaim her husband king.†

Perhaps the most indicative tale of the differing social customs of the Etruscans and the Latin peoples is that of the beginning of the tragic story of Lucretia. The sons of Tarquinius Superbus and other young Roman noblemen were campaigning not far from the city. One evening the subject came up of the relative virtues of their wives and the test was set that they should ride to Rome immediately, and see what each of their wives was doing. When they arrived so unexpectedly, the Etruscan princesses were found at a luxurious banquet, whiling away the time with their young friends, while Lucretia, the Roman wife, sat at home with her maidens, spinning by lamp light. This is certainly a Roman picture of womanly virtue; illustrations of Etruscan ladies with a spindle in their hand do exist, though they are rare.†

The comparative freedom of women within society is well attested by the monuments. Women are shown dining with their husbands, reclining upon the same couch, and also attending the games, sometimes even taking the place of honour. Indeed, such customs scandalized the Greeks, who repeated scurrilous anecdotes of Etruscan immorality. Theopompus, who was said to have had one of the wickedest tongues in antiquity, told of beautiful Etruscan women who exercised naked, who dined with men who were not their husbands, who drank to excess and were so promiscuous that they brought up their children in common, not knowing who the fathers might be. The men felt no shame in committing the sexual act in public and, moreover, enjoyed homosexual more than heterosexual relations.†

Perhaps it should be noted that even Plautus described Etruscan women as earning their dowries by prostitution.† The evidence of the monuments amply demonstrates, however, that Theopompus' charges are no more than salacious gossip. Not only do the funerary inscriptions show a very strong pride in the family but a clear ideal of married love is expressed in the effigies of affectionate married couples, which we see on some of the sarcophagi (35).

It is less easy to defend Etruscan society from accusations of too great a love of luxury and, in the later centuries, of decadence. There can be little doubt that the Etruscan nobles did enjoy ostentatious wealth, both in private and on public occasions or even in military camp. Dionysius describes this reputation: 'For the Tyrrhenians were a people of dainty and expensive tastes, both at home and in the field carrying about with them, besides the necessities, costly and artistic articles of all kinds designed for pleasure and luxury.' †

When, after the conquest, the great families no longer held political power in the cities but had been confirmed in their social position by Rome, it is impossible not to see a confirmation of decadence in the corpulent figures of some of the Hellenistic sarcophagi, which must admit a loss of vitality and vigour. Perhaps one of the most fair opinions we have of the Etruscans is that given by Diodorus, writing in the first century BC: 'In general', he says, 'they have abandoned the valiant steadfastness that they so prized in former days, and by their indulgence in banquets and effeminate delights they have lost the reputation which their ancestors won in war.'†

Our picture of the other classes of society is meagre, though not entirely non-existent. We simply do not know the exact status of the people who worked the land, whether serfs or slaves, nor the manner of freeing a slave or the position he then might hold. Nor do we know who, precisely, were the men who led the social revolt at Bolsena (Volsinii). Yet there was in Etruria, as well as at Rome, a system of clientage, and the *etera* of the funerary inscriptions, found in the great family tombs, were probably clients. The word *lautni*, also found in the funerary inscriptions, may find its closest analogy in the Latin *libertus*, or freedman, and we know something of their occupations and marriages. Beneath these classes were the slaves, of which the Etruscans had many, and who were not buried in the family tombs. They range from the well-dressed musicians and dancers, who we see depicted in the tomb paintings and other monuments, the troop of actors, owned by the king of Veii, the cooks, shown with their names written beside them in the Golini Tomb, down to the anonymous multitudes.†

Occasionally we find a reference to an individual craftsman, like Vulca of Veii, or a professional man, like the priests or the Faliscan schoolmaster, who betrayed his trust. Judging from the votive offerings of terracotta models of limbs, intestines or other parts of the body or of swaddled babies, medicine must have been firmly bound to religion but Theophrastus knew of the medical qualities of Etruria, and the mineral waters were used in antiquity. Dentistry was also carried out, and we have examples of gold bridges and false teeth from the tombs (*104*). It is interesting to recall, particularly in view of the riches the Etruscans carried to their tombs, that the Twelve Tables of Rome, a series of laws dating to the fifth century BC, decreed that the gold joining their teeth was the only form of that precious metal which the Romans might take to the grave.†

104 False teeth with a gold bridge band

We know a little of the physical attributes of the Etruscans. Working from the figures given in funerary inscriptions, it has been estimated that the average life expectancy of an Etruscan, whether a man or a woman, was about forty years; it is also worthy of note that the average height for a man was 1·64 metres (five feet, four and a half inches) and for a woman 1·55 metres (five feet, one inch). Several attempts have been made to establish the ethnic connections of the Etruscans, using methods ranging from the measurement of skulls and skeletons to the study of the blood groups of the present-day inhabitants of the region. None have proved very successful and to gain an impression of the actual appearance of this people, we should go and look at the many portraits from the tombs and, observing the wide difference of physical types, not expect any simplistic conclusions concerning their racial origin.

9

Leisure, language and literature

The Etruscans held annual festivals at which there were con-
tests and, no doubt, athletic sports, which were also conducted
at funerals and other religious occasions. Sports were pursued
for pleasure as well as ritual purposes, together with indoor
games and the performing arts, and these occupations reflect
both the character of individuals and the society in which they
lived.

LEISURE
When Lucius Tarquinius the Elder wished to celebrate the
games at Rome in a manner more splendid than any of his
predecessors, he had wooden stands erected for the audience

*105 Spectators watching games, a scene from the Tomb of the Two-
horse Chariots, Tarquinia*

106 A chariot race shown on a black-figure phiale *in the Royal Scottish Museum, Edinburgh*

and the entertainment was provided 'by horses and boxers, imported for the most part from Etruria'.† Just such a wooden stand is seen in the paintings of the Tomb of the Two-horse Chariots at Tarquinia (*105*), in which animated groups of men and women sit on benches, protected from the weather by an awning, while the games are in progress in the arena below. Some horses are shown about to be yoked and three chariots are ready and being driven sedately past the stands. Later, we may imagine them in headlong race, a moment depicted in some paintings and other art forms (*106*). One tomb painting at Chiusi shows a driver tossed from his chariot and, in the recently discovered Tomb of the Olympic Games at Tarquinia, a horse has fallen, its legs entangled in the reins, while a charioteer, whip in hand and with the reins tied at his back, glances behind him to judge the distance of his rivals.

There is a brief mention of a chariot race at Veii. Tarquinius Superbus had commissioned from the artists of that city a terracotta four-horse chariot to stand upon the roof of the great, new Capitoline Temple at Rome. The sculptors of Veii undertook the task but, when the terracotta was in the furnace, it swelled and hardened in so strange a manner that soothsayers were called in; they predicted that whoever possessed the sculpture should have power and success. The people of Veii therefore decided not to give up the terracotta chariot to Rome and, shortly after this, a chariot race took place at Veii. A charioteer of good birth won the race, which incidentally shows that the nobles took part in the games, and, having received the prize, was walking his horses out of the arena, when they suddenly bolted and galloped until they reached Rome and came to the Capitol. Such a portent persuaded the people of Veii to give up the terracotta chariot to Rome and all that had been foretold came to pass.†

In the arena shown in the Tomb of the Two-horse Chariots, other athletic sports are taking place, carefully judged by umpires. Like those we have already seen with the prizes of bronze bowls stacked between them (*100*), there are wrestlers and boxers, their hands bound with thongs; one athlete flexes his knee, as another gets ready to vault, and discus-throwers wait their turn, while armed athletes prepare for a race or to perform a dance. From other illustrations we know, too, of horse and foot races, of javelin throwing and the long jump, performed in the Greek manner with weights in either hand; indeed, all these athletic sports were taken over from the Greeks.

The Etruscans also performed a ritual or exercise, which the Romans later adopted and called the Troy Game, inventing stories connecting it with ancient Troy. An Etruscan vase, dated to the seventh century BC, shows a maze, marked with the word *truia*, whose precise meaning is not known but may signify an armed dance or the place where this was performed; from this maze, there appear armed dancers and two horsemen. Probably this performance originated in an armed drill or dance for young soldiers and was concerned with the handling of arms and horsemanship.

In the story of the quarrel between Veii and the other states of Etruria in 403 BC the king of Veii suddenly withdrew his troop of actors, who were his slaves, from the festival at the *Fanum Voltumnae*.† There is no direct evidence of exactly what entertainments might have taken place there but we may imagine that, as well as athletic sports, there were other performances, like those we know from the paintings of the Tomb of the Jugglers at Tarquinia or the Tomb of the Monkey at Chiusi. In both these tombs, the principal figure, almost certainly the personage for whom the tomb was made, sits watching the entertainment held in their honour. In the Tomb of the Monkey, which is named after a small monkey seen sitting perched in a tree with a chain dangling from its neck, a cloaked woman is sitting on a high stool, her feet resting on a footstool, while she holds a parasol over her head. Various athletic sports are taking place and a girl juggler is shown, as well as a figure, who is as small as a child but has a beard; this may well be a comic turn, as a similar figure appears on a vase, led by a full-grown man, and next to a boy climbing a pole. In the Tomb of the Jugglers, a girl balances a lighted incense-burner on her head, while a youth stands ready with a disc or ball in either hand. They are about to perform to the notes of a flute player, to whose music a woman is already dancing, gaily dressed and with a bright spot of rouge upon her cheek (*48*).

These must have been enjoyable diversions but Etruscan men were also devoted to the pursuit of game in the country or near the sea coast. There were large game reserves in Etruria and there are many scenes of the chase of deers or boars, hares or birds with the huntsmen either mounted or on foot and often accompanied with a pack of dogs. One may quote illustrations in which deer are hunted with bows (*57*) or boars pursued with a pack of dogs and spears or even an axe; hares are coursed by dogs and clubbed with thick sticks, while a sling shot is aimed at flying birds (*107*). We also see nets set up on poles to ensnare driven game and there is a fascinating description of another Etruscan method of using nets:†

It is said in Etruria, where wild pigs and stags are caught with nets and dogs in the usual manner of hunters, that success is greater when music is used as an aid. . . . Nets are stretched out and all kinds of traps set in position. Along comes an experienced piper. He avoids so far as possible regular melodies and loud sounds and plays the sweetest tunes the double pipe can produce. In the silent solitude, his airs float up to the tops of the mountains, into the gorges and thickets, into all the retreats and breeding grounds of the game. At first, when the sounds reach their ears, the animals are terrified and filled with fear. But later they are irresistibly overcome by enjoyment of the music. Enraptured, they abandon their young, their lairs, their familiar trails from which they would normally be unwilling to stray. Thus the wild beasts of the Tyrrhenian forests are gradually attracted by the powerful music and they draw near, bewitched by the sounds, till they fall overpowered by music, into the snares.

107 Boys at sea in a boat, a painting from the Tomb of Hunting and Fishing, Tarquinia

Some of the tomb paintings especially evoke the Etruscans' delight in this out-of-doors life. The Tomb of Hunting and Fishing is justly famous and presents a charming series of scenes by the coast; a boy climbs the grass covered cliffs, while another dives into the blue sea. A fishing expedition is also taking place; small rowing-boats are at sea, with helmsmen holding the steering oar at the stern; from one boat a man aims a fishing spear, and, leaning over the bow of another skiff, a boy dangles a hook and line into the water (*107*). This was not the only method of line fishing known in Etruria, as a boy, shown on a mirror, holds a rod in one hand and has caught a small fish. One panel of the Tomb of Hunting and Fishing illustrates a return from a successful day's hunting; in front run the dogs, then come mounted huntsmen and behind, attendants carry the dead game, dangling from a pole carried across their shoulders. From the details of the newly discovered Tomb of the Huntsman at Tarquinia, we may imagine the hunters have returned to a pavilion, set up in the country, for here the game is shown hanging from the tent poles, together with a hunter's shady hat, bright red and with cords to tie under the chin.

Even banquets seem to have been held out-of-doors on some occasions, judging from the gay awnings carried on poles, in some of the tomb paintings. Shrubs and trees are also shown, often decked with wreaths and fillets, which were worn at banquets. As well as being part of the funerary rites, banquets were also a focus of social life and Diodorus vividly described such occasions: '. . . twice a day, they (the Etruscans) spread costly tables and upon them everything that is appropriate for excessive luxury, providing gaily coloured couches and silver drinking cups of every description and servants-in-waiting in no small number . . .'†. The habit of dining twice a day seemed indulgent to the Greeks and almost as dubious as banqueting with their wives; in Etruscan scenes, three couches are often shown at banquets, either with men alone or with men and their wives, who are reclining upon the same couch or sitting at the foot of their husband's couch, as the fashion of the age dictated. The Etruscans, like the Greeks, habitually ate with their fingers; as we have seen in the paintings from the Golini Tomb, tables were laden with food and set beside the banqueting couches, while pottery vessels and bronze incense-burners stood on sideboards and the room was lit by candles burning on bronze candelabra (72).

In the illustrations from the Tomb of the Painted Vases at Tarquinia, we may see two fine, black-figure *amphorae* standing on a side table, together with an undecorated *krater*, possibly made of bronze, while underneath there are stacked two pottery *kylikes* upside down. Wreaths, necklaces and a basket or casket hang on the wall; a dog, wearing a collar, lies under a low table, set beside the banqueting couch. A thick mattress covers the couch, on which recline a couple, the only diners shown in this tomb and we may imagine them as a husband and wife at home (*108*). The woman wears a *tutulus*, a necklace and disc ear-rings and holds a wreath in her hand; she is gazing at her companion, who returns the glance and lightly touches her chin with his hand. He is wearing a wreath and holds in his left hand a huge *kylix*, while nearby stands a naked serving boy, two ladles in one hand and a strainer in the other, ready to fill his master's drinking cup.

When more diners are present, the serving boys hurry to fetch the drink from *kraters* and, carrying jugs in their hands, fill

108 A couple reclining upon a banqueting couch, a scene from the Tomb of the Painted Vases, Tarquinia

the cups held out by the guests (*63A, 37*). Music and dancing are a constant feature of the banqueting scenes, and under the couches we may often see pet animals, including dogs and cats, together with birds, which pick up the crumbs. The whole scene is filled with bustle and animation, sometimes a guest is the worse for drink, sometimes, when women are present, there is an atmosphere of 'teasing, prattling and sudden gusts of desire' as Heurgon has described. On other occasions, we see a domestic tranquility, with the children present as the parents dine.

In the fourth century BC and during Hellenistic times, *kottabos* was sometimes played at banquets and there are examples of the special bronze stands used in this game. They have a heavy round base and a slender vertical shaft, rising nearly two metres (about six feet) in height; a large disc was fixed about half-way up the shaft and a second, smaller disc was balanced at the top. The object of this drinking game was to fling the dregs of a wine cup so that they hit the top disc, making it fall and ring on the one below; an Etruscan red-figure cup shows a *maenad* replacing the disc at the top of a *kottabos* stand, while Bacchus, already rather drunk, looks on.

The Etruscans also played dice games and dice may also have been used in fortune telling. Many examples have been found in the tombs; usually they are marked with dots, like modern dice, but one pair has the Etruscan words for the first six numbers written upon their sides. The replica of a gaming board, together with a little bag to hold counters or dice, seen on the wall of the Tomb of the Reliefs has been described; a mirror made at Palestrina shows such a board in use. A young man and woman sit indoors and set in front of them at table height is a board, with clearly marked parallel lines. A short conversation is written beside them in archaic Latin: 'I think I will win', says the young woman and he replies, 'I expect so!'

One of the characteristics of the Etruscans most noted in antiquity was their love of music. They or the Lydians were credited with the invention of the war trumpet and, as we have seen, they had several types of these bronze instruments, which they also used in processions and even to guide their flocks. The Etruscans were particularly famed, however, for their constant playing of the flute, and a flute player is one of the most frequent figures in Etruscan scenes, especially when rhythmic movement was required. Flute players appear at religious festivals, at military parades, at the games, at banquets, in the kitchen and, as we have seen, there was even a story that they could charm wild animals from their lairs. The Greeks noticed this constant accompaniment, saying the Etruscans boxed, kneaded bread and even whipped their slaves to the sound of the flute.†

The favourite type of flute among the Etruscans had two pipes, one pipe fingered in either hand, and flute players are often shown wearing the *phorbeia*, or mouth band, tied round their heads. Single-piped flutes were known and there is an example of a flute held sideways in the mouth, like a modern flute; pan-pipes were played but are usually shown used by satyrs or sirens. Very often the flute was accompanied by the lyre (*49*); the form of these instruments altered down the centuries but they had a sounding box and seven or more strings and were played with the fingers of the left hand on the strings, which were plucked with a *plectron* held in the right hand. Some-times flautists and lyre-players are shown dancing to their own music but more often there are other dancers, some with castanets in their hands.

Martial dancing, performed at the games, has been men-tioned above; dancers armed with weapons and holding shields already appear on an engraved silver vase, dating to the seventh century BC. At an early period, there are also representations of lines of female dancers, their hands linked in a chain, but by the time tomb painting began, dancers are usually shown in pairs or singly. Though we do not know the tunes nor the time of the accompanying music, it has been suggested that they may be dancing to a three-four beat, like that of the *tripudium*, danced by one of the ancient colleges of priests at Rome, in which the foot was stamped three times upon the ground and the leaps were high. Perhaps one characteristic gesture of Etruscan dancers should be noted; great emphasis was placed on the hands and, in this gesture, they are shown with the fingers bent far backwards.

Down to 364 BC, Rome had no public entertainments except the games held in the arena but in that year there was a plague and, when all other propitiations had failed, performers were brought in from Etruria. 'Without any singing, without imitat-ing the action of singers, players who had been brought in from Etruria danced to the strains of the flautist and performed not ungraceful evolutions in the Tuscan style'.† Young Romans began to imitate them and, from the Etruscan word *ister* meaning 'player', they came to be known as *histriones*, a Latin word from which the English 'histrionics' is in turn derived. The *histriones* of Rome began to sing prepared songs as well, but it is a strange fact that the Etruscans do not appear to have prac-tised this art, even to the accompaniment of the lyre, as was common in Greece, or in rustic improvisations like the Fes-cennine songs of the Faliscans. Etruscan singers are not shown in representational scenes and the references we have to singing in Etruria are confined to religious contexts.

So, at least until Hellenistic times, the performing arts in Etruria seem to have been confined to instrumentalists, dancers, masked mimes, and comic actors, though there may, too, have been recitations. Yet, in Magna Graecia, the great Greek plays had been performed in stone-built theatres since the fifth century BC. Theatrical presentations in the Greek manner first came to Rome in the middle of the third century BC, after the Roman army had been campaigning in the south of Italy and, no doubt, had learned to enjoy such spectacles in the Greek cities, but the first stone-built theatres were not constructed at Rome until the first century BC. Though no stone theatres were yet built in Etruria, bas-reliefs dating from the third century BC may reflect the impact of dramatic performances, held perhaps in temporary wooden theatres or in the market places of the towns. We also hear of an Etruscan tragic dramatist who probably worked in the second century BC.

LANGUAGE AND LITERATURE

Etruscan does not belong to the Indo-European family of languages, though it was influenced by them at an early date. The only similar dialect known to us is that found written in a few inscriptions from the island of Lemnos, together with some scattered place and proper names in western Asia Minor.

Such an almost complete lack of comparative material, together with the rarity of bilingual inscriptions, inevitably imposes enormous difficulties upon scholars who try to understand the language. Some have sought comparative material and, even though Etruscan resembles no known language, this has not prevented unsuccessful modern attempts to test the language against Greek, Latin, Hebrew, Ethiopic, Egyptian, Arabic, Coptic, Chinese, Celtic, Basque, Anglo-Saxon, Teutonic, Runic and so on. The great difficulties in understanding the language do not spring from an inability to read the script, every letter of which is now clearly understood. It is as if books were discovered, printed in our own Roman letters, so that one could articulate the words without trouble, but written in an unknown language with no known parallels. In order to begin to decipher the books, the scholar would look for words, like names or titles, which might be recognizable, having crossed from a known language into the unfamiliar tongue, and he would try to find repetitive groups of words and grammatical forms so that he might begin to understand the vocabulary and the syntax of the unknown tongue.

The Etruscans had learned to write by the middle of the

seventh century BC. The name of *Larthia* was written on some of her most precious possessions found in the Regolini-Galassi Tomb, and letters were scratched on some *bucchero* pots. Among the earliest examples of a full alphabet from Etruria is that written along the side of a small ivory writing tablet, which was found at Marsiliana; this has twenty-two letters of a Phoenician or Semitic alphabet, together with four Greek additions at the end (*109*). The Greeks had adopted their letters from the Semitic script and the Marsiliana alphabet was certainly learned from a Greek source; the most likely derivation is from the Euboeans of Cuma, who were closely in touch with the Etruscans at this time. The Marsiliana script is close to the Chalcidian lettering used at Cuma, though it is possible that other sources may also have played a part in forming the early Etruscan alphabet, as the letter *san* is not known to have been used at Cuma.

Etruscan Alphabets

Model	VI–V Centuries	IV–I Centuries	Greek Names of Letters	Modern Equivalents
			alpha	a
			beta	(b)
			gamma	c (k)
			delta	(d)
			epsilon	c
			digamma	v
			zeta	z
			eta	h
			theta	th
			iota	i
			kappa	k
			lambda	l
			mu	m
			nu	n
			ksi (samech)	(s)
			omicron	(o)
			pi	p
			san	ś
			koppa	q
			rho	r
			sigma	s
			tau	t
			upsilon	u
			ksi	s
			phi	ph
			chi	ch

109 The Marsiliana tablet and Etruscan alphabets

It should be emphasized here that the coming of the alphabet to Etruria has nothing whatsoever to do with the problem of the origin of the Etruscans. Rather, the difficulties in assessing all the elements which went to make up the Etruscan alphabet should be seen as another example of the complicated pattern of cultural transmission from the east Mediterranean to Etruria, so often with the Greeks acting as intermediaries.

Languages impose their own requirements upon scripts and so, over the centuries, modifications took place in the Etruscan alphabet (*109*). For example, the Etruscan language needed a letter to express our 'f' and adopted the symbol '8'. However, it did not require all the Phoenician and Greek letters and so, by the fourth century BC, the Etruscan alphabet had been reduced to twenty letters. One of the greatest gifts the Etruscans handed on to their neighbours was the art of writing, and the peoples of northern Italy, from the Oscan-speaking people, including the Samnites of Campania, to the Veneti, living around what is now Venice, learned their letters from the Etruscans. Among these peoples were the Romans.

The Etruscan inscriptions may be read but how may they be understood without reference to a comparative language or languages? There are several approaches. We have a number of glosses, or translations of Etruscan words, mentioned in the works of Greek and Roman authors. Some Etruscan names for the months were known and Livy's statement that the Etruscan word *ister* passed into Latin as *histrio* has been cited, as well as the word *lucumo*, which meant 'king' in Etruscan—though incidentally this title was muddled and given to Lucius Tarquinius as a personal name. Thus, we also know *capu* means 'falcon', *cassis* means 'helmet' and other words, about sixty glosses in all. A story giving a gloss and, we may guess, much in the Etruscan manner, is related by Suetonius: shortly before Caesar Augustus died, lightning struck a monument on which his name was written and erased the first letter 'C'. Since this letter stood for the number one hundred, this was interpreted to mean that Augustus would live for one hundred days more and then join the gods, since '*aesar*' meant 'gods' in Etruscan.†

It is clear that proper names of people or places will remain largely unchanged between two languages; thus we may read the names of cities found in Etruscan inscriptions and know, for instance, that Volterra, Latin Volaterrae, was written *Velathri* in Etruscan and Populonia either *Pupluna* or *Fufluna*. Again, surviving place names may very occasionally help us confirm an Etruscan word; the word *tular* is known from several inscriptions and has been shown to mean 'boundary', so it is interesting to find it recalled in the modern place name of Tollara, near Piacenza, or, derived from the Umbrian form, *tuder*, in Todi, close to the borders between Etruria and Umbria.

There are, too, some bilingual inscriptions, usually Etruscan-Latin, though they are remarkably few in number and generally both short and late; should a long inscription in both languages be found, it would undoubtedly be a major contribution. It must be admitted, however, that the expectations aroused by the discovery of the Pyrgi plaques, with both Punic and Etruscan scripts, were not completely fulfilled, as the translation between the two languages was not close enough to give a definitive correlation for all the Etruscan words.

Often repeated formulae have been unravelled simply by internal deduction; these are mainly inscriptions recording possession, votive offerings or the funerary texts. Of the former, the inscription usually gives the name of the owner, often with the formula 'I belong to . . .'; votives record the name of the person who dedicated the object, and sometimes the name of the god, whilst the funerary inscriptions give names and family relationships, the age and often the offices held by a dead man. From these we know that *puia* means 'wife', *sec* or *seχ* 'daughter' and *ati* 'mother'; for masculine family relationships, it is worth quoting in part the inscription recorded upon the scroll, held by *Lars Pulenas* of Tarquinia (*112*). His genealogy runs as follows: '*Laris Pulenas, Larces clan, Larthal papacs, Velthurus nefts, prumts Pules Larisal Creices*'† and this may be translated 'Lars Pulenas, son of Larce, nephew of Larth, grandson of Velthur, great-grandson of Laris Pule, the Greek'.

Other deductive methods also help; sometimes groups of words are constantly found together in Etruscan and may be matched with similar groups of words from analogous contexts in Umbrian or Latin. Again, a word like *phersu*, written beside a masked figure, which finds a close Latin equivalent in *persona*, may be assumed to have the same basic meaning, whichever way the borrowing took place. Another example is that of the word *hinthial*, which is written close to the name of Tiresias, in a scene in the underworld, painted in the Tomb of Orcus. From a well-known Homeric reference to the 'shade of Tiresias' in the underworld, it has been concluded the *hinthial* means 'shade' or 'soul' in Etruscan.

We also know of Greek words adopted by the Etruscans, and of Greek words which passed through Etruscan into Latin; of these, the names of Greek gods and heroes, often inscribed on mirrors, are particularly important. These words and names give us insight into the sound of the Etruscan language. Further, there are enough inscriptions to permit a rudimentary grammar to be constructed from the observed changes in the case endings of nouns and the tenses of verbs. This brief description of the research into the problems of the vocabulary and syntax of the Etruscan language will show that progress, though limited, is nevertheless apparent. The difficulties are formidable without much comparative material; it is worth recalling that, having no other language by which to test Etruscan, it seemed impossible until recently to reach a general agreement upon the correct order for the names of the first six numbers, though these were known, written in words not figures, upon the six sides of the dice from Tuscania.

Altogether, there are about ten thousand examples of Etruscan inscriptions, spanning from the seventh to the first century BC; many published in the *Corpus Inscriptionum Etruscarum*. The great majority are funerary texts, written on stone or terracotta monuments or upon the walls of tombs; then there are outstanding inscriptions, like the Capua tile, a ritual text, the boundary stone from near Perugia, the Magliano lead disc, with an inscription written in a spiral, the bronze liver from Piacenza, together with the mirrors, votives, some inscriptions on pottery, lead sling pellets, coins and even a pair of dice. All these objects have one thing in common; the inscriptions have been written on imperishable materials. Ordinary writing materials were different. Like the Greeks and Romans, the Etruscans used waxed tablets, often made of wood; these tablets could be single, as in the example from Marsiliana (*109*), or hinged, like that lying open in the hand of a boy on a cinerary chest at Volterra (*110*). The letters were written on the wax with a sharp point or *stilus*, and on the example illustrated here, the youth, decorating the top, carries a tablet in one hand and a *stilus* in the other. Like most Etruscan writing, the script would be written from right to left and the tablets may sometimes be seen held lengthways across the knees; this attitude is clearly seen in a bas-relief from Chiusi, in which a young man is writing on a hinged tablet (*111*); he is sitting on a platform with two umpires at some games and we may imagine that he is recording the names of the winners.

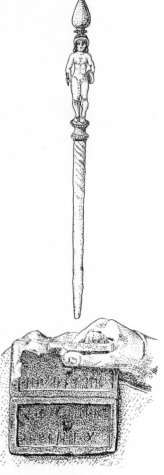

110 Hinged writing tablet and bronze stilus

111 A man writing on a hinged tablet, shown on a bas-relief from Chiusi in the Palermo Archaeological Museum

12 Scroll in the hands of Lars
ulenas *from a sarcophagus in
arquinia Archaeological
Museum*

The Etruscans also used scrolls on which to write; these have
been mentioned above and one may be seen, half unrolled, in
the hands of *Lars Pulenas* on his sarcophagus in Tarquinia (*112*).
This is the *volumen* of the Romans and was a long strip of cloth,
often of linen. The words were written in columns with a reed
or quill in black or red ink; it has been suggested that a small
bucchero pot, with a narrow neck, shaped like a cock and with the
alphabet written upon it, might have served as an ink-well. The
scrolls were kept rolled up, often in boxes, and must have been
an inconvenient method of writing and reading. By an extraordinary stroke of fortune, parts of an Etruscan linen scroll
actually survive; somehow this scroll reached Egypt in antiquity
and was used as the wrappings for a mummy. In the nineteenth
century AD, this mummy was bought by a traveller, who took
it home to Yugoslavia, where it is now in the Museum of
Zagreb; enough may be read to know that it is an Etruscan
religious text, enumerating the rituals to be carried out upon
certain days.

Though Greek and Latin texts were written on just as
perishable materials as those of the Etruscans, much of their
literature has survived, as the languages were known and the
texts were valued and, throughout the Dark and Middle Ages,
the manuscripts were copied and recopied and so have come
down to us. Etruscan, on the other hand, was becoming obso-
lete as a written language by the first century BC and, unless a
text had been translated into Latin, Etruscan literature was
not understood, remained uncopied and has thus disappeared.

We may be certain that the inscriptions we possess on imperishable objects are far from representative of all Etruscan writings and we should ask ourselves just how the Etruscans used their literacy.

Some extant inscriptions have been described, but the ancient sources tell us of other realms of literary activity, which now have vanished. In a famous reference, after speaking of the education of the Roman Consul's brother at Caere (modern Cerveteri) during the fourth century BC, Livy says 'I have authority for believing that in that age Roman boys were regularly . . . schooled in Etruscan literature, as nowadays they are trained in Greek'.† We cannot tell exactly what these writings were, yet the phrase sets a picture of Etruscan learning and the monuments tell us that they were well versed in Homeric and other Greek narrative.

We also hear of Etruscan stories and see some of them illustrated and it is possible that a poetic diction lies behind the rhythm of language discovered in some inscriptions. It is likely funeral speeches were given and, perhaps, written down and we know of Etruscan histories. The recollections of the cities' ancient history, which survived at Tarquinia and Vulci, can probably be attributed to written sources and such records must have been the basis for the twenty volumes, or scrolls, which the Emperor Claudius wrote concerning the Etruscans. We hear, too, of a writer on agricultural affairs with an Etruscan name and of an Etruscan dramatist, who was probably working in the second century BC.†

Yet the extant monuments and all we have learned of the Etruscans should prepare us for the fact that it was for their religious literature that the Etruscans were famous in antiquity. Here, the references are more prolific and we hear of *Libri Tagetici* and *Libri Vegoici*, containing the revelations of Tages and Vegoia, of the *Libri Haruspicini* and *Libri Fulgurales*, concerning divination and the *Libri Rituales*, which included formulae for worship, dedication and the ritual division of time and space. Yet, neither from the written records nor from the monuments do we learn of records of other affairs of life; we do not know whether the Etruscans had written laws, treaties or other political decrees or administrative regulations, commercial lists and contracts. It cannot be overestimated how this imbalance of the literary evidence, whether it springs from an accident of survival or from the characteristic usage of Etruscan life, has affected our view of this people: we have but a feeble, and perhaps distorted, echo of the living voice of the Etruscans.

Conclusions

It has been possible to describe many aspects of Etruscan life, the geographical setting and the historical background, the development of art and the objects used from day to day by the Etruscans, to catch a glimpse of their military, economic, political and social forms and to grasp some idea of the spiritual and practical nature of their thought. Yet it must not be forgotten how incomplete is our knowledge and how wide the void left by the loss of their literature; without it, we must sketch the manner of their lives from the material remains and the voices of their rivals. How, then, may we sum up the personality of the Etruscans and their achievement in the broad current of European history?

Their successes were many and varied. In the great age of colonization in the west Mediterranean, the people of northern Lazio and Tuscany retained their lands and, gaining from the rich mineral resources available to them, welcomed the trade offered by the Greeks and merchants of the east Mediterranean. An extraordinary transformation took place. The Etruscans proved themselves capable of assimilating both the knowledge and the arts brought to them by these contacts and, during the seventh century BC, Etruria herself emerged as a Mediterranean civilization. For over four hundred years, she was an educating influence among her Italic neighbours and goods created by her craftsmen were carried beyond the Alps, there to affect the native styles.

The sixth century BC saw the height of Etruscan power; the Greeks told tales of her prowess at sea and the Romans remembered her as a formidable foe. Had we Etruscan records, they might have recounted adventures on the high seas and in new lands and told of victories and triumphs won by warrior kings and the proud spirit of queens, granted the gift of prophesy. It was a brilliant archaic age and, though the few sources available to us cannot fill out the evidence of the material remains, yet the Etruscans appear at this time to have been particularly attuned to the world around them and to have possessed a full confidence, which we see reflected in their art.

Towards the end of the sixth century BC, however, we hear of military and naval defeats and soon the Etruscans abandoned their expansive policies; by the end of the fifth century, the city-states had assumed a defensive attitude and even begun to seem old-fashioned. Set in a traditional mould, they did not respond to the intellectual revolution in the Greek world nor the gradual encroachment upon aristocratic government, which was being tested at Rome; they were unable, in the great struggle between Rome and Veii, to adopt new methods to combat an unprecedented and dangerous situation. While the young Roman Republic was already finding her genius for social compromise and the slow assimilation of neighbouring peoples, the exclusive societies of the Etruscan cities remained unchanged. The nobles continued their virtually absolute rule but maintained their pride in family and city, their deep religious lore and perceptive patronage of the arts, which contributed so much to the community. They did not, however, learn to combine the city-states when need arose nor to heal the division between the classes. Though it is idle to speculate whether the Etruscans, with all their resources centralized, could have withstood the attacks of the Samnites in Campania, the Gauls in the Po Valley, the Greeks at sea and the rising tide of Roman power, yet it is necessary to note the sadly few attempts to unite the strength of the Etruscan cities and the reports of revolutionary strife.

After the loss of their independence, the Etruscans showed a continued dignity of life; traditional customs were followed, contemporary artistic styles were appreciated and local forms maintained. But to a people deeply believing that the gods ordained the course of human events, their defeat must have brought a double despondency; at this time, their art assumes a subjective mood, dwelling on suffering and the after-life. Power had left the cities and large areas of the countryside were in serious decline; in this atmosphere, some of the gibes of late Republican writers may well be based on fact. Other Romans, however, remembered their city's ancient debt: under the rule of Etruscan kings, Rome had first acquired an urban prestige, which helped to lay the foundations for her future rôle as mistress of the Mediterranean world; from the Etruscans, Rome had received some of her most cherished rites and ceremonies and learned many practical lessons. Above all, it was from the Etruscans, with their deep and sustained love of Hellenic art, that the peoples of central Italy had first gained a consciousness of Greek forms. Though it is not always easy to decide in which direction the cultural currents were flowing, it is certain that the example of Etruria gave Rome her earliest appreciation of Greek art. Later, when they had conquered the Greek world, the Romans were deeply influenced by the civilization of Greece and this, in turn, did much to preserve it for posterity.

It may well be that these were the Etruscans' most direct contributions to European civilization. For later centuries, it was perhaps not entirely a coincidence that the rebirth of art came about in much the same region as that of ancient Etruria. One has only to think of the charming comparison between an Etruscan terracotta and Donatello's head of St George, or of Michelangelo's sketch of Hades, taken from some Etruscan tomb, and recall that Benvenuto Cellini restored the beautiful bronze statue of a Chimera, found at Arezzo in AD 1553, to know that the artists of the Renaissance were not unaware of the Etruscan inheritance. Such wealth as the Etruscans left might well help to prime a new inspiration; it evoked a fresh enthusiasm in the scholars and excavators of the eighteenth and nineteenth centuries, whose discoveries, in their turn, enriched the museums of the world. In our own century, it has brought a harvest of finely illustrated books, so that now, between the museums and libraries, we may all share something of the Etruscan achievement and feel the vitality in the life of the Etruscans.

NOTES

(1) In references to the early centuries, the clumsy term 'northern Lazio and Tuscany' has been used to equate with the region which was later to become Etruria, since this name cannot be correctly used before the seventh century BC. It should be noted that parts of modern Umbria also lie within ancient Etruria. It is almost impossible to be consistent in the usage of place-names and the writer hopes to have achieved a general clarity, rather than a strict uniformity. Since it has been assumed that the reader will not necessarily be familiar with the works of Latin authors and because it may prove helpful to travellers in Italy, modern Italian place-names have generally been used in this book with their Greek or Latin equivalents in brackets, where it seemed necessary, or used, where the sense demanded it. Exceptions to this general rule have been made, principally where there is no close modern equivalent to a place or region, or when a Latin or an English name is so familiar that it seemed pedantic to the writer to use another form.

(2) Both Greek and Latin authors used various spellings for their names of the Etruscans: here, Tyrrhenians and Tusci or Etrusci have been used throughout.

(3) Unless otherwise stated, all dates in this book are BC.

(4) The writer wishes to give a word of warning about Chapter 2. In this Chapter, so many conflicting theories are discussed that some qualifying adverbs, essential in other circumstances, have been omitted. 'Probably' and 'perhaps' repeated too often only serve to disrupt the text and muddle the argument, which is presented here as it appears to the writer.

(5) The names of Etruscan tombs are sometimes descriptive, sometimes given in honour of the owner or discoverer and occasionally local nicknames. Where possible, these names have been translated from the Italian.

(6) The term 'Magna Graecia' has been used in the expanded sense to include the Greek city-states of both southern Italy and Sicily.

SHORT GLOSSARY

For the names and usage of the pottery forms, see page 100*f*.

Augur. Soothsayer or diviner; member of a priestly college at Rome and an expert in interpreting the will of the gods, chiefly by the observation of the flight of birds.

Bucchero. Name given to the distinctive black pottery with a glossy finish made by the Etruscans.

Cippus. Funerary monument set up near a tomb, either plain or carved and of many forms.

Cuniculus. Underground passage cut through the rock; frequently found in southern Etruria and Lazio.

Fascis (pl. *fasces*). The bundle of rods with an axe carried before a Roman magistrate as a symbol of authority.

Fibula. Brooch or safety-pin, often richly decorated.

Fossa (pl. *fosse*). Trench grave, associated with the burial of the corpse by inhumation.

Haruspex (pl. haruspices, haruspicy). Soothsayer or diviner and the method of interpreting the will of the gods by the examination of the entrails, and in particular the liver, of sacrificed animals.

Hoplite. Heavy-armed, Greek infantry-man.

Impasto. Term used for a wide variety of Italic pottery made with impure clay, usually fired brown/black.

Lituus. Curved stick, associated with Etruscan priests and Roman augurs.

Necropolis. Cemetery; city of the dead.

Podium. Stone base of a temple or other monument.

Pozzetto (pl. *pozzetti*). Well grave, associated with the cremation of the dead and the placing of the ashes in urns.

Situla. Name frequently used for bronze buckets.

Stele (pl. *stelai*). A term often used to describe an upright stone slab, carved in bas-relief, set up as a funerary monument.

Tumulus. Mound of earth or stones covering a tomb or tombs.

SELECTED BIBLIOGRAPHY

GENERAL

Banti, L. *Il Mondo degli Etruschi*, 2nd Edition (1969). A detailed account of the Etruscan cities, stressing their individuality. It includes an excellent Bibliography of the literature on the Etruscans.

Bloch, R. *The Etruscans* (1958), Thames and Hudson. This book includes a history of Etruscology.

Boethius, A. *et al. Etruscan Culture. Land and People* (1962). There are many very fine photographs of the sites and the countryside in this book.

Nogara, B. *Gli Etruschi e la loro Civiltà* (1933). A good summary of Etruscan civilization.

Pallottino, M. *Etruscologia*, 6th Edition (1968). Published in English by Penguin Books (1955) and Allen Lane (1970). A brilliant all-round description of the Etruscans and their language.

Richardson, E. *The Etruscans, their Art and Civilization* (1964), Chicago University Press. A general account, including many valuable observations on Etruscan art and architecture.

Scullard, H. H. *The Etruscan Cities and Rome* (1967). Thames and Hudson. The cities are described individually and their relationship with Rome traced.

Strong, D. *The Early Etruscans* (1968), Evans Bros. An up-to-date account of the Etruscans to the end of the fifth century BC.

Von Vacano, O. W. *Die Etrusker: Werden und geistige Welt* (1955), Stuttgart. Very finely illustrated.

ARCHAEOLOGY

Hencken, H. *Tarquinia and Etruscan Origins* (1968), Thames and Hudson. A detailed description of the early cemeteries of Tarquinia and a fine summary of the problem of Etruscan origins. This book is a shortened version of Hencken's major contribution in *Tarquinia, Villanovans and Early Etruscans* (1968), Peabody Museum, Massachusetts.

Montelius, O. *La Civilisation Primitive en Italie depuis I'Introduction des Métaux* (1895–1905), Stockholm, 5 Vols. This indispensable work on Italian prehistory also illustrates many Etruscan objects.

Randall-MacIver, D. *Villanovans and Early Etruscans* (1924), Oxford. This book is now out of date but it describes the archaeological background of most important sites in Etruria.

See, too, the annual publications of *Monumenti Antichi* and *Notizie degli Scavi*, both begun in the last century, *Studi Etruschi*, first published in 1927 by the *Istituto di Studi Etruschi e Italici* in Florence and the publications of the foreign Academies in Rome.

ANCIENT TEXTS
See the Loeb editions, with translations, of the ancient historians and commentators.

HISTORY
Etruria
Fell, R. A. L. *Etruria and Rome* (1924), CUP. A full account of the known history of Etruria.
Phoenicians
Harden, D. *The Phoenicians* (1962), Thames and Hudson. This book includes chapters on the colonial expansion in the west Mediterranean and Carthage.
Western Greeks
Woodhead, A. G. *The Greeks in the West* (1962), Thames and Hudson.

TOPOGRAPHY
Dennis, G. *The Cities and Cemeteries of Etruria*, 3rd Edition (1883). First published in 1848, this book remains an unsurpassed guide to Etruscan sites; it has many illustrations and a sustained enthusiasm and accuracy.
Lawrence, D. H. *Etruscan Places* (1932).
Solari, A. *Topografia storica dell'Etruria* (1915–20). Pisa.

Of all the many available guide-books, the most detailed are the regional volumes of the *Guida d'Italia* of the Touring Club Italiano. The volumes on *Lazio, Roma e Dintorni, Umbria, Toscana* and *Firenze e Dintorni* cover the area of ancient Etruria.

ART AND ARCHITECTURE

Ducati, P. *Storia dell'Arte Etrusca* (1927). A most instructive pioneer book.

Giglioli, G. Q. *L'Arte Etrusca* (1935), Milan. An indispensable series of illustrations of Etruscan culture.

Mansuelli, G. *Etruria and Early Rome* (1966), Methuen. A misleading title for a sensitive book on Etruscan art.

Moretti, M. and Maetzke, G. *The Art of the Etruscans* (1970), Thames and Hudson. A superb assembly of illustrations of Etruscan places and objects.

Pallottino, M. *Etruscan Painting* (1952), Geneva. Well-reproduced illustrations in colour and a discussion on Etruscan tomb painting.

Pallottino, M. *Art of the Etruscans* (1955), Thames and Hudson. A book of illustrations on the full range of Etruscan art with comments.

Patroni, G. *Storia dell'Architettural. Architettura Etrusca* (1941), Bergamo. See for an introduction to Etruscan architectural forms.

Riis, P. J. *Tyrrhenika: An Archaeological Study of Etruscan Sculpture of the Archaic and Classical Periods* (1941), Copenhagen.

Riis, P. J. *An Introduction to Etruscan Art* (1953), Copenhagen.

SPECIALIZED SUBJECTS
Pottery

Beazley, J. D. *Etruscan Vase-Painting* (1947), Oxford.

Cook, R. M. *Greek Painted Pottery* (1960), Methuen. The author describes the Etruscan types of pottery, which followed Greek forms.

Bronzes

Gerhard, E. *Etruskische Spiegel* (1840–97). The most comprehensive publication of Etruscan mirrors.

Lamb, W. *Greek and Roman Bronzes* (1929), Methuen. Etruscan bronzes are often mentioned and may be compared with contemporary works.

SELECTED BIBLIOGRAPHY

JEWELLERY
Becatti, G. *Oreficerie antiche* (1955), Rome.

IVORIES
Huls, Y. *Ivoires d'Etrurie* (1957), Brussels.

COINS
Cesano, S. L. *Tipi monetali etruschi* (1926), Rome.

EVERYDAY LIFE
Heurgon, J. *The Daily Life of the Etruscans* (1961), Weidenfeld and Nicolson. An incomparable book, which gives a wide and vivid view of Etruscan life.
Solari, A. *Vita pubblica e privata degli Etruschi* (1931), Florence. Few aspects, illustrative of Etruscan life, have been omitted.

RELIGION
Grenier, A. *Les Religions étrusques et romaines* (1948), Paris.

LANGUAGE
Pallottino, M. *Elementi di lingua etrusca* (1936), Florence.
Pallottino, M. *Testimonia Linguae Etruscae* (1954), Florence. This gives many useful inscriptions.
Staccioli, R. A. *La Lingua degli Etruschi* (1970), Rome. A summary and discussion of the language.

ANCIENT AUTHORS AND
ABBREVIATIONS

Aelian. Claudius Aelianus. Lived second century AD.

Aeschylus. Greek tragic dramatist and poet. Lived sixth and into fifth century BC.

Anticleides. Greek historian. Probably lived end of fourth or third century BC.

Aristotle. Greek philosopher. Lived fourth century BC.

Arnobius. Christian apologist. Lived end of third century AD.
    Adv. Nat. *Adversus Nationes*, a defence of Christianity.

Arrian. Arrianus. Greek historian and philosopher. Lived second century AD.

Athenaeus. Greek grammarian. Lived third century AD. Wrote *Banquet for the Learned*, which includes many extracts from the ancient authors.

Ausonius. Decimus Magnus Ausonius. Latin poet. Born c. AD 310.

Cato. M. Porcius Cato, often surnamed the Censor. Lived 234–149 BC. Wrote *Origines*, a work which has not come down to us but dealt with early Italian history.

Catullus. Valerius Catullus. Latin poet. Lived first century BC.

Censorinus. Roman scholar. Lived third century AD.

Cicero. M. Tullius Cicero. Famous Roman orator and philosopher. Lived 106–43 BC.
    de Div. *de Divinatione*, a discussion on the methods of divination.

CIE *Corpus Inscriptionum Etruscarum.*

CIL *Corpus Inscriptionum Latinarum.*

Diod. Sic. Diodorus Siculus. Greek historian. Lived first century BC. Wrote a Universal history.

D. of H. Dionysius of Halicarnassus. Greek historian. Lived first century BC. Wrote *Roman Antiquities.*

Ephorus.   Greek historian. Lived fourth century BC. His works are lost but are quoted in subsequent authors.

Festus.   S. Pompeius Festus. Roman grammarian. Lived (?) second century AD.

Florus.   L. Annaeus Florus. Roman historian. Lived second century AD.

Gellius.   Aulus Gellius. Roman grammarian. Lived second century AD.

Hellanicus of Lesbos.   Greek historian. Lived fifth century BC.

Herod.   Herodotus. Great Greek historian. Lived fifth century BC.

Hesiod.   Greek epic poet. Lived (?) eighth century BC.

Homer.   Greek epic poet. Lived (?) ninth century BC.

Horace.   Q. Horatius Flaccus. Latin poet. Lived 65–8 BC.

Isidore of Seville.   Grammarian. Lived seventh century AD.

Justin.   Justinus. Historian. Lived second century AD.

Livy.   Titus Livius. Great Roman historian. Lived 59 BC– AD 17.

Macrobius.   Aurelius Theodosius Macrobius. Grammarian. Lived about AD 400.
>   *Sat.   Saturnalia Convivia.*

Martianus Capella.   Satirist. Lived (?) fifth century AD. Wrote *de nuptiis Mercurii et Philologiae.*

Pausanias.   Greek traveller and geographer. Lived second century AD. Wrote *Itinerary of Greece.*

Pherecrates.   Greek comic poet. Lived at the end of the fifth century BC.

Pindar.   Pindarus. Greek lyric poet. Lived end of sixth into fifth century and died 442 BC.

Plautus.   T. Maccius Plautus. Latin comic poet. Died 184 BC.

Pliny.   Gaius Plinius Secundus. Pliny the Elder. Lived AD 23– 79.
>   *NH   Naturalis Historia,* an encyclopedia of the natural sciences and many other subjects.

Plutarch.   Greek historian and philosopher. Lived late first and early second century AD. Wrote *Parallel Lives,* the biographies of eminent Greeks and Romans.

Poly.   Polybius. Greek historian. Lived second century BC.

Propertius.   S. Aurelius Propertius. Latin poet. Lived end of first century BC.

Rutilius Namatianus.   Latin poet. Lived fifth century AD.

Sallust.   C. Sallustius Crispus. Roman historian. Lived 86–34 BC.

    Cat.   Catilina.

Seneca.   L. Annaeus Seneca. Philosopher and writer of tragedies. Died AD 65.

    Quaes. Nat.   Quaestiones Naturales.
    Consol. ad Helv.   de Consolatione ad Helviam.

Servius.   Servius Honoratus. Roman grammarian. Lived at the end of the fourth century AD.

    ad Aen., a commentary on Virgil's *Aeneid*.

Silius Italicus.   Latin poet. Lived first century AD.

Strabo.   Greek geographer. Lived first century BC and on into first century AD. His work, *Geography*, includes a description of Italy.

Suetonius.   C. Suetonius Tranquillus. Biographer. Lived end of the first and second century AD. Wrote *Lives of the Twelve Caesars*.

Tacitus.   C. Cornelius Tacitus. Roman historian. Lived in first and early second century AD.

TLE   Pallottino, M., *Testimonia Linguae Etruscae* (1954).

Theophrastus.   Greek philosopher and natural historian. Lived fourth century BC.

    Hist. Pl. History of Plants.

Theopompus.   Greek historian. Lived fourth century BC.

Thucydides.   Great Greek historian. Lived fifth century BC.

Valerius Maximus.   Roman historian. Lived first century AD.

Varro.   M. Terentius Varro. Great Roman scholar. Lived 116–28 BC.

    de L.L.   de Lingua Latina.
    de R.R.   de Re Rustica.

Virgil.   P. Virgilius Maro. Latin poet. Lived 70–19 BC.

Vitruvius.   M. Vitruvius Pollio. Lived towards the end of the first century BC.

    de Arch.   de Architectura, a treatise on architecture.

Xanthus.   Lydian historian. Lived fifth century BC. Wrote in Greek.

Zosimus.   Historian. Lived fifth century AD.

LIST OF DATES

BC	ETRURIA AND THE WEST MEDITERRANEAN		GREECE AND THE EAST MEDITERRANEAN
Ninth century		? Phoenician sailors in the western Mediterranean Villanovan I in northern Lazio and Tuscany	Geometric period in Greece
			Euboean trading posts established in the Levant
	814	Traditional date for the foundation of Carthage	
Eighth century		Villanovan II in northern Lazio and Tuscany	
	c. 760	Euboeans settle on Ischia	
	733	Foundation of Syracuse	Assyrians advance to the Mediterranean coast
	c. 725		Protocorinthian pottery *Orientalizing style*
	c. 700	Phoenicians settle in west Sicily and Sardinia	
Seventh century	c. 675	Bocchoris Tomb Orientalizing style begins in Etruria First Etruscan inscriptions Demaratus of Corinth at Tarquinia	Phoenician cities under pressure from the Assyrians
	616– 578	Traditional dates for reign of Lucius Tarquinius the Elder at Rome	
	c. 600	Etruscan colonial expansion into Campania Foundation of Marseille by Phocaeans	

203

BC	ETRURIA AND THE WEST MEDITERRANEAN	GREECE AND THE EAST MEDITERRANEAN
		Archaic style
Sixth century	Carthage becomes an imperial power in the west Mediterranean	
c. 565	Phocaeans found Alalia in Corsica	c. 570 Attic black-figure pottery of mature style
c. 535	Battle of Alalia; Corsica falls to Etruscans and Carthaginians hold Sardinia	546 Persians defeat Lydia and subdue Ionian cities
		c. 530 Attic red-figure pottery begins
c. 525	Etruscan colonial expansion into lower Po Valley begins	
524	Aristodemos of Cuma defeats Etruscans in Campania	
510	Fall of Sybaris	
509	Traditional date for the expulsion of Tarquinius Superbus from Rome	
	Republican era begins	
	Campaigns of Porsenna	
Fifth century		499 Ionian Revolt
		490 Battle of Marathon
480	Battle of Himera	480 Battle of Salamis
474	Hieron of Syracuse defeats Etruscans at sea off Cuma	*Classical style*
	Gauls begin to settle in Po Valley	431– Peloponnesian War 404
435	Fidenae taken by Rome	
423	Capua captured by people of Samnite hills	
414– 413	Athenians besiege Syracuse; Etruscans send ships	
405	Siege of Veii begins	
Fourth century	396 Veii captured by the Romans and ? Gauls take Melpum in the Po Valley	

BC	ETRURIA AND THE WEST MEDITERRANEAN	GREECE AND THE EAST MEDITERRANEAN
391– 390	Gaulish raid south of the Apennines; battle of Allia and burning of Rome	
384	Pyrgi sacked by Dionysius of Syracuse	
c. 383	Sutri and Nepi, Latin colonies, founded in former territory of Veii	
358– 351	Tarquinia and other cities fight Rome	
351– 311	Forty-year truce between Tarquinia and Rome	323 Death of Alexander *Hellenistic style*
327– 304	Second Samnite War	
311– 310	Combined Etruscan cities besiege Sutri. Romans advance over Ciminian range	
302	Revolution in Arezzo against Cilnii family	
Third century c. 280	End of the independence of the Etruscan city-states	
280– 275	Pyrrhic War	
273	Cosa, Latin colony, founded in former territory of Vulci	
265– 264	Revolution at Bolsena (Volsinii)	
264– 241	First Punic War	
241	Revolt of Civita Castellana (Falerii Veteres)	
225	Romans, with Etruscan allies, defeat Gauls at Talamone	
218– 201	Second Punic War; Hannibal in Italy	
205	Scipio's levy	

BC	ETRURIA AND THE WEST MEDITERRANEAN	GREECE AND THE EAST MEDITERRANEAN
Second and first centuries	196 Slave revolt in Etruria	
	90– 88 Social War and grant of Roman Citizenship to the Etruscan cities	
	82 After the Marian War, Sulla takes citizenship from Volterra and Arezzo	
	44 Death of Julius Caesar	
	42 Perugia besieged and burnt in Civil War	
	27 BC– AD 14 Reign of Augustus	
	Imperial era begins	
	AD 41– 54 Reign of Claudius	

REFERENCES

Passages in the text containing information derived from ancient authors are denoted by †. Details of these sources are as follows:

PAGE

12 (1) Strabo V, 4, 4: Livy VIII, 22.
13 (1) Thucydides VI, 3–5.
16 (1) Herod., I, 94.
   (2) Hellanicus, quoted by D. of H., I, 28.
17 (1) See Anticleides, quoted by Strabo V, 2, 4: Pliny, *NH*, III, 50: Tacitus, *Annals*, IV, 55. Seneca, *Consol. ad Helv.*, VII, 2.
   (2) D. of H., I, 5 and I, 28 ff.
18 (1) Livy V, 33: Pliny, *NH*, III, 133: Justin XX, 5.
   (2) Thucydides IV, 109.
19 (1) Herod., I, 173.
24 (1) Ephorus, quoted by Strabo VI, 2, 2. Hesiod, *Theogony*, 1010–1016.
26 (1) Pliny, *NH*, XXXV, 152.
27 (1) Livy I, 34.
   (2) *CIL*, XIII, 1668.
29 (1) Livy IV, 37.
   (2) Strabo V, 4, 8–V, 4, 13: Pliny, *NH*, III, 70.
   (3) Servius, *ad Aen.*, X, 198.
30 (1) Livy, V, 35: Livy V, 33. Cato, followed by Servius, *ad Aen.*, XI, 567.
   (2) Thucydides I, 13: Herod., I, 170: Aristotle, *Politics*, III, 5, 10; 1280 a.
31 (1) Herod., I, 166–167.
   (2) D. of H., VII, 3–4.
   (3) Livy II, 9 ff.
32 (1) Livy II, 14: D. of H., VII, 5 f.
   (2) Herod., VII, 166.
   (3) Diod. Sic., XI, 20 ff.
   (4) Diod. Sic., XI, 88.
33 (1) Livy V, 17.
34 (1) Livy V, 1 ff.
   (2) Livy V, 33: Diod. Sic. XIV, 113: Pliny, *NH*, III, 125.

PAGE

34 (3) Strabo V, 2, 8: Diod. Sic., XV, 14.
35 (1) Livy V, 33.
   (2) Livy V, 33 ff.
36 (1) Arrian VII, 15, 4.
   (2) Livy IX, 32: Livy IX, 36 f.: Livy IX, 41: Diod. Sic., XX, 35.
37 (1) Livy X, 4, 5, and 12: Poly., II, 20.
38 (1) Gellius XI, 7, 4.
42 (1) Strabo V, 2, 3.
44 (1) Livy V, 49 ff.
   (2) Propertius IV, 10, 27.
45 (1) Varro, quoted by Pliny, *NH*, XXXV, 157.
47 (1) Livy VI, 9.
   (2) Strabo V, 2, 2.
49 (1) Pliny, *NH*, II, 139: XXXIV, 34.
   (2) Livy V, 31.
54 (1) Plutarch, *Life of Tiberius Gracchus*, VIII, 7.
   (2) D. of H., III, 51.
56 (1) Livy II, 34.
58 (1) Livy IX, 37.
59 (1) Vitruvius, *de Arch.*, II, 8, 9: Pliny, *NH*, XXXV, 173.
60 (1) Poly., II, 25: Sallust, *Cat.*, 24.
   (2) Pliny, *NH*, III, 120: Strabo V, 1, 7.
62 (1) Festus 358 L: Plutarch, *Life of Romulus*, XI.
63 (1) Servius, *ad Aen.*, I, 422: Vitruvius, *de Arch.*, I, 7, 1.
68 (1) Vitruvius, *de Arch.*, IV, 7 and III, 3, 5.
70 (1) Vitruvius, *de Arch.*, III, 3, 5.
73 (1) Vitruvius, *de Arch.*, VI, 3, 1.
   (2) See Varro, *de L.L.*, V, 161: Diod. Sic., V, 40.
77 (1) Pliny, *NH*, XXXV, 152.

PAGE
78 (1) Pliny, *NH*, XXXV, 154 ff.
91 (1) See Pliny, *NH*, XXXV, 17 ff.
109 (1) Kritias, quoted by Athenaeus I, 28 b. Pherecrates, quoted by Athenaeus XV, 700 c. Horace, *Epistulae*, II, 2, 180.
128 (1) D. of H., III, 61.
135 (1) Diod. Sic., V, 40: Livy I, 43: Aeschylus, *Eumenides*, 567.
137 (1) Livy II, 9 ff.: D. of H., IX, 19: Livy IV, 20: Livy V, 36: Livy VII, 17.
138 (1) Livy I, 43: Diod., Sic., XXIII, 2.
139 (1) D. of H., IX, 5: Livy IX, 36: D. of H. VII, 3: Livy X, 10: Livy IX, 29 and X, 16: Diod. Sic., V, 40.
140 (1) D. of H., I, 25: Pliny, *NH*, VII, 209: Livy V, 33: D. of H., I, 11: Strabo VI, 2, 2: Diod. Sic., V, 9, 13 and 20: Ausonius, *Epistles*, XXXI, 236: Diod. Sic., XX, 61.
      (2) Pausanias V, 12, 5.
141 (1) Pliny, *NH*, XXXIV, 34.
146 (1) Diod. Sic., V, 13.
147 (1) Livy XXVIII, 45.
      (2) Livy IX, 36: Theophrastus, *Hist. Pl.*, V, 8: Strabo V, 2, 5: Pliny, *NH*, XIV, 9.
148 (1) Pliny, *NH*, III, 120: Livy V, 15.
149 (1) Diod. Sic., V, 40: Varro, *de R.R.*, I, 44, 2: Pliny, *NH*, XVIII, 67: Pliny, *NH*, XVIII, 87: Livy IX, 36.
150 (1) See D. of H., I, 37.
      (2) Poly., XII, 4.
      (3) Strabo V, 2, 6.
152 (1) Livy V, 1.
153 (1) Seneca, *Quaes. Nat.*, II, 32, 2.
      (2) Cicero, *de Div.*, II, 50.
154 (1) See Livy V, 15: XXVII, 37: XXXV, 21: XXXVI, 37. Cicero, *de Haruspicum responsis*, passim.
      (2) Cicero, *de Div.*, I, 92–93: Pliny, *NH*, II, 138 ff.
155 (1) Martianus Capella, *de Nuptiis Mercurii et Philologiae*, I, 45: Caecina, quoted by Seneca, *Quaest. Nat.*, II, 39, 1 and II, 41: Varro, quoted by Arnobius, *Adv. Nat.*, III, 40.

PAGE
157 (1) Livy VII, 3: Varro, *de L.L.*, V, 46.
158 (1) Cato, quoted by Cicero, *de Div.*, II, 52: *CIL*, XI, 5265: Zosimus V, 41.
      (2) Festus 358 L: Tacitus, *Histories*, IV, 53.
160 (1) Livy, Epitome of Book XVI: Athenaeus IV, 153.
      (2) Pausanias X, 28, 7 ff.
161 (1) See Livy IV, 23: V, 1: V, 17.
162 (1) See Livy V, 33: D. of H., VI, 75: Diod. Sic., XIV, 113.
163 (1) Macrobius, *Sat.*, I, 15, 13.
164 (1) Livy I, 8: Silius Italicus, *Punica*, VIII, 483 f.: Florus I, 1, 5: D. of H., III, 61.
165 (1) Livy I, 8: Diod. Sic., V, 40.
166 (1) Livy V, 1.
      (2) *TLE*, 324 and 325.
167 (1) Valerius Maximus IX, 1: Florus I, 16, 21.
168 (1) *TLE*, 136.
      (2) Livy I, 34, 41 and 46 ff.
      (3) Livy I, 57.
169 (1) Theopompus, quoted by Athenaeus XII, 517 d f.
      (2) Plautus, *Cistellaria*, II, 3, 20 ff. This may be based on Herodotus' account of Lydian customs, see Herod., I, 93.
      (3) D. of H., IX, 16.
      (4) Diod. Sic., V, 40.
170 (1) Livy V, 1.
      (2) Livy V, 27: Theophrastus, *Hist. Pl.*, IX, 15, 1.
173 (1) Livy I, 35.
174 (1) Plutarch, *Life of Publicola*, XIII.
      (2) Livy V, 1.
175 (1) Varro, *de R.R.*, III, 12, 1: Aelian, *de Natura Animalium*, XII, 46.
177 (1) Diod. Sic., V, 40.
179 (1) Athenaeus XII, 518 b.
180 (1) Livy VII, 2.
183 (1) Livy VII, 2: Servius, *ad Aen.*, II, 278: X, 145: Isidor XVIII, 14: Suetonius, *Caesar Augustus*, XCVII.
184 (1) *TLE*, 131.
188 (1) Livy IX, 36.
      (2) Pliny, *NH*, XXXVI, 93: Varro, quoted by Censorinus XVII, 6: Suetonius, *Claudius*, XLII: Varro, *de L.L.*, V, 55.

INDEX

Numerals in heavy type refer to the figure-numbers of illustrations

209

INDEX

Faliscans, 33–4, 46, 49, 102, 143, 170, 180
Family, *see Gens*
Fanum Voltumnae, 157–8, 161, 174
Fascis, 163–4, 195; **101**
Felsina, *see* Bologna
Fibula, 9, 11, 23, 123–5, 157, 195; **5A, 75, 76**
Fidenae (modern Fidene), 33, 45
Fiesole (Faesulae), 60, 70, 162
Fish, fishing, 150, 176
Florence (ancient Florentia, Italian Firenze), 60, 143
Archaeological Museum, 50, 53, 55, 74, 151; **29B, 40, 44, 72, 81, 83, 93**
Flute, flautist, 87, 151, 158, 175, 179–80
Food, 149–51, 177
Forest, 1, 36, 140, 145, 147
Fossa, 195; *see* Grave
Freedman, 170
Fruit, 35, 149–51
Funerary practice and rites, 5–9, 18–20, 31, 42, 44, 55, 56, 94, 158–60, 184–185, 188; **99, 100**
Furniture, 118–22, 145, 147

Games; *see* Athletics, Funerary practice
Gateway, 46, 47, 54, 58, 62, 63, 66; **19, 24**
Gauls, Gaulish, 18, 29, 33–9, 58, 60–1, 88, 127, 134, 137, 139, 142, 191, 204, 205
Gens (pl. *gentes*), 138; 166–70
Glass, 118, 123, 125; **70A**
God, goddess, 152–61
Gold, goldwork, 109, 118, 123–7, 141, 142, 145, 164, 170; **75, 77**
Government, 161–7
Grain, 56, 102, 147–9
Grave, 7–9, 40–61; *see* Funerary practice, Tomb
Greek geometric art and pottery, 11–12, 23, 75, 102

Hair-style, 115, 127–30
Hannibal, 38, 58, 205
Haruspicy, 19–20, 38, 153–4, 157–8, 188, 195; **96**
Hat, 128, 157, 176, 177
Hellenistic period and artistic style, 25, 38, 51, 52, 53, 60, 66, 70, 72, 73, 87–91, 97–8, 108, 121, 127, 129, 136, 142, 144, 149, 178, 180, 205
Helmet, 9, 23, 32, 46, 122, 131–7, 147, 183; **4, 10, 81, 82, 83**
Hercules (Etruscan Hercle), 82, 156, 160
Hieron of Syracuse, 32, 204
Himera, 13, 32, 204
Horse, 7, 94, 96, 144, 173–4

Horse-gear, 9, 21–3, 136, 145, 173; **6A**
House, 44, 45, 48, 52, 53, 65, 72–4, 91, 100, 160
Household goods, 100–22
Hunting, 150, 175–6; **57, 107**
Hut, 7–8, 48, 72, 160; **2**
Hydria, 101, 106, 110, 115; **52, 57**

Impasto, 9, 102–3, 195; **54A**
Imperial period, 38, 52, 54, 58, 60, 162, 206
Incense-burner, 112, 175, 177; **63B**
Industry, 53–4, 145–8
Inhumation, *see* Funerary practice
Inscription, Etruscan, 17–18, 38, 59, 91, 115, 157, 166, 167, 181–9, 203
Inscription, Latin, 47, 58, 184
Inscription, Punic, 32, 184
Ionia, Ionian, 29, 30, 77, 81, 94, 106, 125, 128, 204
Iron, ironwork, 3, 5, 11–13, 53, 123, 131, 141, 145–7, 164
Iron Age, 9, 23, 34
Ischia (Pithecusae), 4, 12, 20, 32
Isola Farnese, *see* Veii
Italocorinthian pottery, 105; **56**
Ivory, 75, 105, 115, 118, 120, 124–5, 164, 182; **74, 78**

Jewellery, 9, 115, 122–7
Juno (Etruscan Uni), 63, 155
Jupiter (Etruscan Tin, Tinia), 45, 63, 154, 155

Kantharos, 101, 141; **52**
Kiln, 66, 103, 145
King, 27, 31, 33, 136, 138, 140, 162–4, 168, 170, 183
Kitchen, 151; **93**
Krater, 102, 108, 110, 121, 139, 177; **52, 60, 86**
Kottabos, 115, 178
Kylix, 101, 177; **52**

Language, Etruscan, 11, 18, 36, 38, 58, 181–9
Language, Greek, 63, 149, 185
Language, Indo-European, 5, 11, 18, 181
Language, Latin, 11, 33, 118, 153, 155, 156, 158, 160, 179, 180, 183, 184
Lars Porsenna, 31, 56, 136, 204
Lars Pulenas, 167, 184, 187; **112**
La Tène, 34, 142
Latin colony, 47, 52, 205
Latin peoples, 27, 31, 32, 39, 168
Lazio, northern, 1–13, 15, 18, 20, 24, 26, 190, 193

211